MW01029070

Confidence in Conflict for Sports Officials

Practical Tips for Staying Out of the Cross Fire and Keeping Peace During the Game

By: Pete Jaskulski

Truths Publishing
Milwaukee, WI

Dedication

This book is dedicated to my mom and dad, Marcey and Bob Jaskulski.

Dad treated every player, coach, official and parent with dignity by showing them respect. Thanks for showing us how to do it.

Mom understood the importance of athletics in the lives of her husband and sons. She supported us unconditionally.

Thanks

I would like to express my gratitude to Dave Simon and Bill and Heidi Dittmar for their assistance in the editing of this book.

I would also like to thank all of my umpiring partners who work so hard to respect the game of baseball.

Finally, I would like to thank my wife Pam and my kids, Alex and Kayla. Pam was an accomplished college soccer player. Alex was a three-sport high school athlete and an accomplished college baseball player and now is coaching baseball. Kayla is a three-sport athlete who is working hard as a softball player.

They provide me with great stories to tell.

Copyright © 2015 Vistelar Group

All rights reserved. No part of this publication or its ancillary materials may be reproduced in any form (photocopy, digital file, audio recording) or transmitted by any means (electronic, mechanical, Internet) without prior written permission of the publisher – except as brief, referenced citations imbedded in articles or reviews.

www.ConfidenceInConflict.com

For bulk-purchasing pricing, please contact:
Vistelar Group
1845 N. Farwell Ave., Suite 210
Milwaukee, WI 53202
Phone: 877-690-8230
Fax: 866-406-2374
Email: info@vistelar.com
Web: www.vistelar.com

Pete Jaskulski
Confidence In Conflict For Sports Officials / Pete Jaskulski
ISBN 13: 978-0-9909109-5-4
ISBN 10: 0-9909109-5-4

LCCN: 2015947919

BISAC Subject Headings:
SPORTS & RECREATION / General

Published By Truths Publishing, Milwaukee, WI
Printed In the United States of America

Table of Contents

Forward 1

Preface 5

Introduction 11

Chapter 1 17
Be Alert and Decisive / Respond, Don't React (Be Ready and Stay Safe)

Chapter 2 25
Five Maxims of Communications (Respect Everyone)

Chapter 3 35
Showtime (Get Yourself Ready To Manage The Game)

Chapter 4 43
Universal Greeting (Set The Stage For Collaboration)

Chapter 5 53
Beyond Active Listening (Pay Attention So You Can Respond)

Chapter 6 67
Redirections (Handle The Outbursts Professionally)

Chapter 7 73
Ethical Intervention: Bystander Mobilization (Intervene To Prevent Bad Behavior)

Chapter 8 83
Persuasion (Keeping The Players And Coaches In The Game)

Chapter 9 91
When Words Alone Fail (When Is It Time To Act-Eject or Sanction)

Chapter 10 97
Review and Reporting (Improve Everyone's Performance)

Chapter 11 105
Conclusion (How Do We Improve Our Performance?)

Appendix 1 109
Tips On How To Practice The Skills

Appendix 2 113
Examples of Drills or Activities

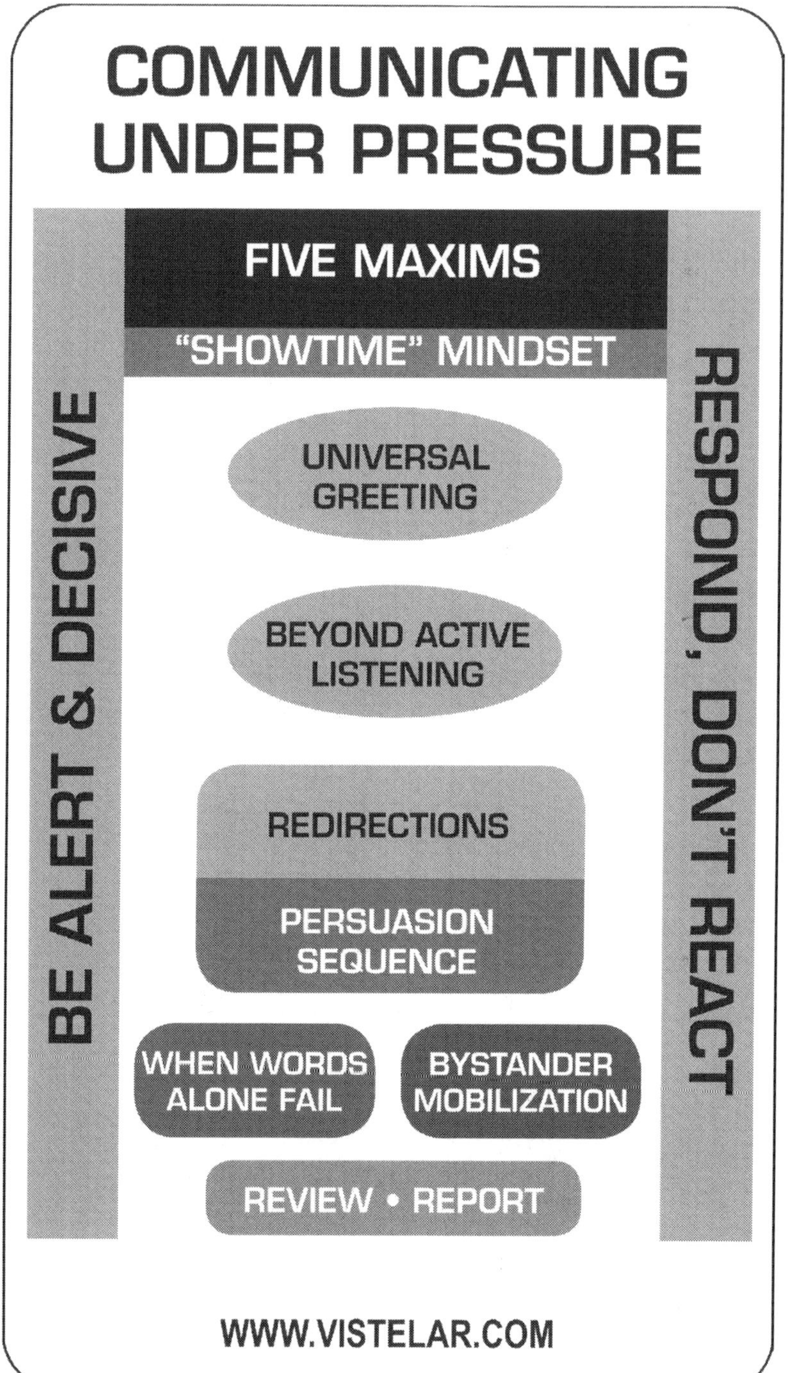

COMMUNICATING UNDER PRESSURE

FIVE MAXIMS

"SHOWTIME" MINDSET

BE ALERT & DECISIVE

RESPOND, DON'T REACT

UNIVERSAL GREETING

BEYOND ACTIVE LISTENING

REDIRECTIONS

PERSUASION SEQUENCE

WHEN WORDS ALONE FAIL

BYSTANDER MOBILIZATION

REVIEW • REPORT

WWW.VISTELAR.COM

Forward

A common thread that flows through those that choose to officiate is a desire to give back, a yearning to take on something impossible to master and a passion for the game they have chosen to officiate.

Many people outside the world of officiating often look funny at those who do it thinking, "There must be something wrong with them for putting themselves in such a horrible position" or "Why would anyone ever want to be an official?"

So is it all worth it? For some, very quickly the answer becomes no and most often relates to their inability to effectively deal with CONFLICT. Their officiating career often stops before they were really even close to enjoying the real benefits of true camaraderie, mental and physical fitness and deep internal satisfaction.

I have spoken to senior officials in many sports and each verified that this is true in their sports as well. The attrition rates are often so high that many never really make it through to the "promised land" where officiating becomes much more predictable through experience, much easier to manage and way more enjoyable.

So *what if* all referees had a greater understanding of conflict: its sources, its characteristics, its outcomes and resolutions? *What if* officials could better master how to control the inevitable conflict which is present in all levels of sports competitions? *What if* they were taught tried and true "Diffusing Techniques" and had "Preplanned Practiced Responses?" Well, I submit many more would make it to that "promised land" where the true rewards of officiating are attainable.

I first met Pete at a regional training camp for a select group of youth and amateur soccer referees in Washington State. This group was comprised of many of the officials who had shown promise and who had the desire to learn more and move up the levels. I was invited there, like Pete, to share experiences of how to better handle the demands of refereeing and to conduct some field training sessions focused around verbal and non-verbal communication. I was told by the camp organizer, Will Nichols, that there was a great speaker who was an expert in conflict resolution and who travels all around the country empowering companies, managers, leaders and sports officials to better deal with conflict.

I was there to instruct and mentor, but I was also there to learn myself. You see, although I had already been blessed with the opportunity to be a High School Varsity Soccer Coach for 30 years and a Major League Soccer Referee for 20 years, I know there is always so much more to learn. One of the greatest things about officiating is that while you can get really good at it, you can never master it!

So there I sat in the audience, feverishly taking notes on every part Pete was covering. What was amazing to me is that while many of his stories related to officiating baseball and other sports, the exact things applied to soccer. All throughout my notes I made short insertions of experiences from my own life that totally related to what he was teaching. One that jumps right out to me is his description of "It's Showtime" and his reference to the differences between the normal face you wear for most of life and your "Game Face" or "Professional Face" that you must selectively activate as an experienced official.

This same thing happened at both of Pete's sessions that I attended and at dinner that night. I had to meet this guy and share with him the many things I found fascinating. That night I discovered Pete's experience as a police officer and coincidentally my Dad had been a police officer for over 36 years. Talk about the importance of "Conflict Resolution" needed by all those in law enforcement! Maybe that is one of the reasons I went into officiating... it seemed much easier than following my Dad's footsteps and trying to do it as a police officer.

So *what if* we all became better at handling conflict? How much better would our marriage and relationships at work be? Would many of life's unexpected conflicts have better and quicker resolutions? Would we walk around better able to handle the stress caused by unpredictability and conflict?

The beauty of reading and applying the concepts and techniques contained in this book is that I believe it will help everyone in life and not just those in officiating. These are life skills...actually they are survival skills.

My life has been greatly enhanced because of sports. The roles of player, coach and official have always been important components in making me who I am today and I now believe that because of all that I have learned from Pete in his talks and in this book that I am better empowered to take all three roles to the next level. My "promised land" has just gotten better and yours will too.

Start flipping the pages, read it over and over and help all those around you by sharing and applying these principles in your everyday life.

Thanks Pete!!!

Bill Dittmar

- 20+ year official in Major League Soccer, NCAA soccer official since 1989
- 30+ years coaching High School Boys Soccer
- Lifelong soccer player from age 7
- Founder of Executive Lifestyle Magazine
- Devoted and always learning as a husband since 1996

Preface

In the mid 1990's, I was umpiring in the private school's state championship high school baseball tournament in Wisconsin. We had a three-person crew and I was assigned to third base. In the fourth inning we had an interesting play happen that generated quite a bit of controversy. With runners on first and third there was a soft line drive single to right field. The runner from first was rounding second base attempting to go to third. The right fielder made a throw to third base in attempt to get the runner. The call at third would be the responsibility of the home plate umpire, my good friend and a good umpire, Tony Klappa. I looked at Tony to see if he was moving to third to make the call. Our eyes met and Tony began hustling to third. The ball was going to beat the runner for what should have been an easy "out" call. That's what happened and Tony made the call. I watched the ball come past me (my responsibility was second base) and moved my focus to second base. I then turned back to third to see a cloud of dust and a ball lying on the field. The third base coach pointed toward the ball to get Tony's attention; he was walking back toward home plate. Tony turned, saw the ball and the ground and reversed his call. All havoc broke loose. The coaches were yelling the crowd was yelling and the players were jumping up and down. I was confused because the third basemen had a ball in his hand. I then realized that a ball had fallen out of Tony's ball bag when he made the out call. I talked to Tony and we figured it out. We then informed the third base coach that the call was "out" (just like the first time). He wasn't happy, but after an explanation he accepted the call. We had restored order and the game continued. I couldn't have invented this story up if had to.

On any Saturday afternoon in America you can bet that there are soccer, basketball, football or baseball games (as well as many other sports) being played somewhere. Athletics is and will continue to be an integral part of our society. Children and adults are participating daily in all kinds of sports. Society is consumed with athletics on all levels professional and collegiate athletics down to youth sports. As the old ABC Wide World of Sports saying goes "the thrill of victory and the agony of defeat" is taking place thousands of times a day. With the "thrill" and agony" comes conflict; similar to what occurred in the baseball game. So what is conflict in sports and how do we handle it? First, let's define it.

Webster defines conflict as an open clash between two opposing groups or individuals. Whether it's youth, high school, collegiate or professional sports, conflict is inevitable. This conflict occurs between players, coaches, parents, fans and even officials. If the conflict is managed properly, the game continues in a respectful, competitive manner. It's the athletic official that assumes the role as the decision-maker, mediator and arbiter. It will be their job to manage that conflict. But how do we accomplish that? That's the challenge for officials. The answer is to understand why people behave in a certain way that may generate conflict during a game. Once we understand the behavior, we can develop a plan that contains the essential communications to improve performance under stress. To improve skills under stress, we have to practice them, and then apply them on the baseball, softball, lacrosse, football and soccer fields, and basketball and volleyball courts. This book takes the reader on a "Conflict Confidence" journey, building your knowledge base, sharing stories and experience to help sports officials (and others) better prevent and manage conflict situations. My hope is this book will help you not only become a better sports official, but also a better person in your day-to-day life: equipping you with additional tools to defuse situations that could detonate.

I've been involved in athletics most of my life, playing baseball into my college years, coaching youth baseball and basketball and umpiring for 33 years. When I grew up, there wasn't a sports season (basketball, baseball and football) that one of my family members was not involved in. My father, Bob, was a public school teacher for 40-plus years. He played basketball at Marquette University after World War II and coached freshman basketball there after he graduated. He coached football, baseball and basketball during his teaching years and is in the Wisconsin Basketball Coach's Hall of Fame. I have four brothers (I'm in the middle) and every one of them played sports and coached in the college, high school, grade school or youth sports level. All of our children have played sports in grade school, high school and college.

There are many families out there just like mine. They value the positive attributes that athletics instills in a young person. These attributes include discipline, teamwork, and the importance of preparation, accountability, sacrifice and hard work. Others argue that athletics, if not managed and coached properly, instills unacceptable behavior and needs to be curtailed. In either case, athletics are not going away. Therefore, we as sports officials need to develop an understanding of why, during a game, people behave a certain way. This behavior may lead to conflict. We also have to develop the skills to manage that conflict in an effective manner so that the athletic experience continues to teach positive values and life lessons.

In my career as a baseball umpire, I worked little league, high school and all divisions of college baseball with umpires of all degrees of skill. I've often asked this question of my colleagues, "What makes a good umpire a great umpire?" Here are just some of those answers: "We have to know the rules"; "we have to be in position to make the calls"; and "we have to be impartial". These answers are all important traits for a good umpire (and there are others). As a matter of fact, these traits are important for all officials regardless of the sport they officiate. So what is an even stronger answer? I believe that the trait that makes a good official a great official is learning how to communicate under pressure so that we can handle the inevitable conflict that will occur.

My goal with this book is to provide the help through the introduction of tactics to prepare the aspiring new athletic official for the inevitable conflict that occurs during an athletic event as well as to enhance the communications skills of experienced officials. So for those of you new to officiating, let's get the sponge ready so you can soak it all in. For those of you already officiating, let's open our minds and consider other options. The goal for every athletic official should be to "disappear in the game." In other words, don't become the focus of the event. It's not about us.

Introduction

I have had the distinct pleasure of teaching the Verbal Defense & Influence courses to diverse organizations throughout the United States, presenting to law enforcement agencies, corrections, and government agencies such as the Transportation Security Administration, Oregon Department of Agriculture, the United States military and the San Luis Obispo Transit Authority. The list of people and organizations continues to grow. This list also includes utility companies, realtors, health care and education organizations. Each organization faces the challenge of communicating with people that are experiencing conflict.

My challenge in writing this book is to reach across all sports and be able to explain the concepts of proper verbalization relative to the sport you officiate. The good news is that these concepts apply to all sports. The universal factor is "conflict." The terminology used in these different sports may vary. The words "game," "ejection" and "foul" may mean different things in different sports. In making references and giving examples, I am going to simplify things by referring to an event as a "game."

Have you been around people who complain about the coaches, parents, fans and even the players in youth sports (or any level of sport)? You may have been the one complaining. There are good officials that leave officiating because they become frustrated with the behavior of the people involved in the sport. I want to keep those people from leaving by giving them the tools to manage the conflict they experience while officiating.

When I speak to sports organizations, I reference a CNBC report from January 2014 that states that youth sports has become a 7 billion dollar industry in travel alone. People are spending their money in sports outside of school-related activities so their kids can develop in their sport of choice. Understanding what is at stake for the players, coaches and parents (fans) is the first step in learning how to manage the conflict. My wife and I have spent a lot of money for our two kids to participate in baseball, softball, soccer, football and basketball. We expect the people who officiate in those events to work as hard as our kids do during each game. We expect the officials to treat the players, coaches and fans with dignity by showing them respect. The officials can play a big part in the development of the young people involved in these sports by modeling the proper behavior during the sporting event.

Regardless of what sport we want to officiate, or at what level we want to officiate, we have to become skilled at communicating with people in crisis while we are under pressure. If we don't have this skill, it's going to be a long game. What help can we give you? It's called Verbal Defense & Influence (VDI) for Sports Officials.

After retiring from my career as a captain for the Milwaukee County Sheriff's office, I became a Training Consultant for Vistelar, which is a global speaking and training organization focused on addressing the entire spectrum of human conflict, from interpersonal discord, verbal abuse and bullying to crisis communications, assault and physical violence. Verbal Defense & Influence (VDI) is a component within Vistelar. During my law enforcement career, I was heavily involved in training and VDI was one of the programs I taught and utilized. At that time, I also umpired high school and college baseball. The skills I used to communicate effectively as a deputy sheriff translated into officiating. I started to make the connection every time I walked in between the lines on the field (even before and after the games).

After making the connection, I began teaching the concepts to new and experienced umpires which solidified the connection. As a training consultant, I then had the opportunity to speak and teach the VDI skills to soccer officials. This was my chance to apply the skills outside of the world of baseball umpiring. Those sessions solidified my belief that the conflict occurring in sports crosses over from sport to sport, and the tactics and skills taught in VDI are applicable in sports (and other life situations) outside of baseball.

The goal of our VDI program is to help the sports official achieve the following:

- Enhance professionalism;
- Decrease complaints from stakeholders in the sport (coaches, players, fans, league commissioners, assigners);

- Lessen the stress involved in dealing with conflict;
- Teach you how to articulate your decisions which can assist in your evaluations by supervisors;
- Increase your morale -- keep officiating fun.

The VDI program will teach you the skills needed to communicate effectively under stress. Therefore you will have a better chance of preventing conflict (between everyone) during the event. It also helps you reduce the chance of any emotional or physical violence that may occur. You will officiate effectively in the midst of stress. In the world of digital media, how you come across to others is tremendously important and can affect your career. The VDI program better prepares you to be ready at all times to handle people and situations more effectively. If someone YouTube's your game or Snapchat's, Tweets or Instagram's an incident, you are demonstrating the best possible skills and appearance for others to see. That reflects well on you, your position as a sports official, your supervisor and the conference or league you work in. Our program enhances your ability to communicate calls and decisions. If social media is reporting your game, you are ready.

In understanding the reason people behave in a certain way during a game, the first thing officials need to understand is that there are "Four Great American" questions that people will ask those in positions of authority:

1. Why (did you make that call)?
2. Who are you (to tell me what to do)?

3. Where do you get your authority (to make that call)?

4. What's in it for me (you cost me...)?

This is the first step in understanding why coaches, players and fans react emotionally. They want answers. The tactics taught in VDI assist the officials in providing the answers without interrupting the flow of game. The goal is to achieve compliance, cooperation and collaboration (3 C's) during the game. We call these the 3 C's.

The VDI program can be divided into ten concepts:

1. Be Alert and Decisive/Respond, Don't React to Conflict;

2. The Five Maxims of Communications;

3. The "Showtime" Mindset;

4. The Universal Greeting;

5. Beyond Active Listening;

6. Redirections;

7. The Persuasion Sequence;

8. Bystander Mobilization;

9. When Words Alone Fail;

10. Review and Reporting.

We will explain and break down each concept with examples of their applications in sports officiating.

Chapter 1

Be Alert and Decisive / Respond, Don't React

(Be Ready and Stay Safe)

To officiate a game effectively, we have to remain alert, be decisive and have a pre-planned practiced response to conflict in mind. Have you ever seen an official that doesn't seem to be concentrating during a game? S/he may be checking a cell phone (I've seen that too many times). Or they're talking to a fan during play or during a break in the action. The hands in the pockets and the arms folded across their chest are also some signs of boredom, fatigue and being disinterested. You might say, "I do that but that doesn't mean I'm not ready to officiate." That's debatable. That type of body language gives the players, coaches and fans an impression that you're not ready, you're disinterested and lazy. There is always someone watching what you do. By giving an impression that you are ready, you are engaged and you care, you positively impact your ability to communicate effectively. To better understand the concept of "awareness" during a game, we utilize a color code that assigns a color to each level:

- White - You are unaware of what's happening (talking to fans, watching another game, checking your messages on your phone);
- Yellow -You are aware of the game situation (penalty kick, runners on base, time left on the clock, conflict between teams/ players);
- Orange - You are in position and ready to make that call, you're aware and ready to prevent the conflict between players or handle that conflict related to a call you have made;
- Red - You make the call, handle the conflict correctly and with professionalism;
- Black - You panic and make a bad decision or react unprofessionally.

As an official you should be in condition yellow, ready to make the call so you can move up to orange. Level orange means you are in position to make the call. You then move up to red, which is where you make the decisive call and/or decision. If you end up in condition black you are in trouble. This is when the conflict occurs and is not handled properly. This happens when you are not paying attention to what is happening during the game (everywhere around you).

In 2014, I had the privilege of teaching VDI at the referees academy hosted by the Washington Soccer Referee's Committee. I attended the breakout sessions, one of which was taught by Major League

Soccer Official Bill Dittmar. Bill ran a drill in which he staged a 3 on 3 soccer game in a confined (much smaller field) area. No running was allowed and all of the players had to constantly communicate with each other just like they would in a game. There was a lot of talking going on. The area was surrounded by the other trainees in groups of two. One official in each group was told to face the field with their eyes closed and try to describe to their partner what was happening on the field -- things like which team had the ball, were they attacking or defending, was there a foul, a goal, etc.? He called this the "Sounds of the Game." The purpose of the drill was to pay attention to what is being said and done on the field, giving you a better feel for the game. In other words, listen not just with your ears but also with all of your senses. I was impressed. This is a concept that I had been teaching to umpires for several years. By listening to what the teams are saying, how they are relating to each other and what the coaches are saying to the players and officials, you can prepare yourself for any type of conflict that will occur. This helps you predict that there will be conflict, prepare you to handle the conflict and justify your response to the conflict.

Let's take a look at a low frequency but high-risk area of officiating. How and why are sports officials physically assaulted? It's because they moved in too close to the player, fan or coach. Dave Young is one of the co-founders Vistelar and the founder and director of ARMA Training and US Fighting Systems. He is one of the nation's leading tactical instructors. Dave created the 10-5-2 rule to understand the importance of distance when communicating with people. At 10 feet we are generally at a safe distance (providing the person is unarmed). At this distance we are assessing the person to determine if moving in closer would be safe. You are looking for signs of excessive emotional attention (yelling, screaming, profanities), and non-verbal cues that may indicate a possibility of assault. If your assessment indicates that you can move in closer, then you do so. At 5 feet you begin to communicate with the person. This may be an introduction (Universal Greeting will be discussed later) or you may be sanctioning the person (calling a foul, an ejection, a yellow/red card). At 2 feet you may have a conversation with a player or coach regarding a call or ruling you have made. It is important to understand that the closer you move towards a person (or they move towards you) who is exhibiting aggressive and/or emotional behavior, the more unsafe the situation becomes.

Here's a scenario: In a soccer game, a player receives a yellow card for a reckless tackle. The player has a reputation for aggression toward officials and other players and has demonstrated this during the game. The soccer official sees another serious foul committed by this player and then runs toward the player holding up a red card. The official moves into the 2-foot zone and gets punched in the face after presenting the card. This kind of bad tactic by officials can and has happened in other sports. Don't move into that danger zone unless you are sure it's safe and only move in if you feel it's absolutely necessary.

There are times when communications will take place inside that 2-foot zone. There are also times when distance is determined by the other person who moves into your zone. What do you do then? When you make an assessment that someone is upset and may make physical contact with you, you should have your hands up to protect yourself. The best tactic is to have your hands above your waist (generally chest level) with open palms. The key here is to appear as non-aggressive as possible without sacrificing your ability to protect yourself. You can practice this tactic by having someone move quickly toward you (arguing a call). You simply place your hands out in front of you and say "Stop, what's the issue?" You can also add in the "time out" sign.

Another tactic that many officials use today is what we call the "thinker's stance." You place a hand on your chin and the opposite hand on your elbow. This position gives an impression that you are listening, which conveys empathy. It also keeps your hands up to protect yourself without showing aggression. There are many other tactics that can be learned but it is important to understand that whatever tactic you use to stop the person from moving aggressively towards you needs to be "meshed" with talking. Meshing is simply combining a physical skill, such as the "thinker's stance," with proper verbalization skills. You don't train each one of these skills separately. Combining them has more impact on the person learning the skills.

Each sport has its own conflicts that can repeat from game to game. In baseball, it may be arguing balls and strikes, in soccer it may be offside calls, in basketball it may be traveling, in football it may be holding calls. Whatever sport, you hear similar things being said from coaches and players. So why do we have officials saying and doing unprofessional things in response to what is being said to them? It's because they over-react to what is said. The rule to remember in these situations is to "stop reacting and start responding" instead.

If we can predict what will happen after a close call at first base or a holding call on a "big" play, then we should have a planned response. If we know that players, coaches and fans have been upset with us during the game, then we should plan our exit from the event. Your plan has to be thought out and practiced to be effective. As "Coach" Bob Lindsey says, instead of practicing "if then" thinking, you should practice "when then" thinking. "If then" thinking portrays a mindset that says "if this happen I will do plan A, B or C." This puts you into a state of denial ("if") that any conflicts will occur during the event. If you practice "when then" thinking, you are simply saying that certain calls you make will provoke certain reactions. When that happens, be ready to respond with plan(s) A, B, C or even D. You will be utilizing a preplanned practiced response.

I conducted training for Transportation Security Administration (TSA) supervisors at one of the largest and busiest airports in the United States. Most of the students supervised the checkpoints at this airport. This is an area where the TSA agents have thousands of contacts with people on a daily basis. In preparing for the training, I asked them to send me a list of the worst things said to their agents during a shift. They sent me two pages of quotes that I considered verbal assaults. We spent a great deal of time scripting responses to these assaults that they hear on daily basis. The teaching point is to create your own scripts to handle the verbal assaults and outbursts. These scripts will ensure that you respond professionally when you're under stress. We'll talk about how to do this in the Redirection chapter.

Chapter 1 Learning Points

- **Remain Alert:** By remaining alert you become aware of everything that is happening during the game. It will helps you make the right call during the game, giving the impression you are in contact with the game and the participants involved. Remaining Alert aids you in predicting when conflict may occur. This allows you to prepare your response to the conflict and prepares you to handle it effectively.
- **Have a Pre-planned Response To Conflict:** There are many people that can demonstrate their ability to communicate effectively with people in a static situation. But can they do it when they are under stress, such as a taut athletic contest? Professionals effectively handle stress and don't lose control when they have a pre-planned response to conflict.
- **10-5-2 Rule:** Any time you move within 10 feet of an angry person, your ability to react to an assault decreases. The 10-5-2 rule gives you a visual impression of the importance of when to make your assessment of someone's behavior at an appropriate distance. The 10-5-2 rule keeps you safe by reminding you that as you get closer to an angry person your hands need to come up to protect yourself. Remember to keep those hands up, in an open position, with your palms out. This conveys "stop" and also gives an impression that you are open to discussion. By utilizing a "thinker's stance" you are keeping your hands up and conveying that you are listening. This helps to convey "empathy".

- **Meshing:** Communicating effectively under stress is like swinging a bat, shooting a basketball, or kicking a soccer ball. They are all psychomotor skills. It takes 3,000 to 5,000 repetitions of a skill for it to become permanent. Therefore, the more you practice the skill (the right way), the more proficient you become. Mesh your skills when you practice your skills. Combine the appropriate Verbal Defense & Influence tactic with a physical skill. By meshing the skills you will become more proficient at communicating while under stress. Meshing embeds the skills into your memory.

Chapter 2

Five Maxims of Communications (Respect Everyone)

In teaching VDI to officials, I have encountered different age groups, different races, different ethnic groups and officials from different sports. Officials encounter the same types of people. All sports include different ages, races, genders and ethnic groups. Officials need to be skilled in communicating with all of these different groups of people. Sounds like a daunting task. But instead of concentrating on how different everyone is in each sport, VDI teaches the Five Maxims of Communications that reach across all ages, races, genders and ethnic groups. The first rule, which is unconditional, is to treat people with dignity by showing them respect. Every skill discussed in this book evolves from this unconditional rule. The rest of the Maxims are as follows:

1. Listen With All Your Senses;

2. Ask, Don't Tell Someone To Do Something;

3. Explain Why They Are Being Asked-Set Context;

4. Offer Options Not Threats;

5. Give A Second Chance.

So let's break these down relative to officiating. The first rule is unconditional. Treat the players, coaches and fans with dignity by showing them respect. The good official understands that this must occur regardless of the other person's behavior (this doesn't mean you don't sanction or eject when it is appropriate). Take this quote from the North Dakota Highway Patrol: "We treat people like ladies and gentlemen, not necessarily because they are, but because we are." If you disrespect people, you lose control. You will become the focal point of the conflict because you lost control. Your call or decision may have been correct but no one will care because they will see you as disrespectful towards others. You can sanction someone while still showing them respect. We'll discuss this later in the book.

One of the greatest ways to show respect before, during and after the game is to acknowledge and listen to what the coaches and players are saying. Some sports allow more time than others to listen to the players and coaches. If you don't have much time (because the flow of the game doesn't allow it), simply acknowledge that you heard them and let them know you can talk to them when there is a break in the action. In many instances they just want you to hear what they have to say.

You start the process of showing respect by being open to listening to the coaches and players. The following story illustrates this point. I was the base umpire for a spring high school baseball game.

The spring in Wisconsin is rough on baseball players. It was about 40 degrees, with the winds gusting at nearly 35 miles per hour. The wind was blowing in from right field. As the base umpire, I had to make several close calls at first. I called a runner out at first on a close judgment that completed a double play. This was the third close play that didn't go the way the team on offense wanted. It was the third out in the inning so after I made the call I began to run to short right field where I stand between innings. I was running right into the wind. While running, I checked over my shoulder to see if the coach was going to come out and discuss the call. He was, so I turned to meet him halfway. He was running in slow motion because of the strong wind. His hat then blew off and he chased it, picked it up and waved at me as if to say "I give up." He then went back to the dugout. I laughed to myself not in disrespect but because it was funny. He's a good coach and very professional. I wasn't going to make him run out to me because of the wind. That would have been disrespectful. We talked later. I told him that I was going to meet him half way. He said it was too hard to run into the wind so he just decided it wasn't worth the trip.

Listening is not just hearing. It also involves your other senses. Watch the other nonverbals that occur on the field/court and bench area. Instead of daydreaming or checking the messages on your cell phone, pay attention to what is being said and done in the bench area and on the fields and courts. This doesn't mean you have "rabbit ears" (responding to every little thing that is being said). Are the teams showing aggression toward each other? Are the coaches frustrated with the performance of their team? Are the players frustrated with the coaches? These are just some of the indications that conflict may occur (so you can prepare yourself and possibly prevent any conflict).

The next four Maxims are all conditional based on the behavior of the person you are talking with. In other words, if the coach or player says or does something unacceptable, then you have to act (maybe an ejection). There are ramifications for people who violate the rules of conduct and sportsmanship. We are not saying that you need to stand there and listen and not respond accordingly. Do what you have to do.

Athletic events involve spectators. These spectators include parents, friends and other family members. These athletes are performing in front of crowds large and small, and there is usually someone at the event supporting them. This puts some pressure on the players and coaches. No one likes to fail, especially in front of the people that support them. Therefore don't be surprised when a player or coach postures during a game. The posturing can be magnified even more when they feel that they are being disrespected, especially in front of a crowd. The posturing may take the form of defiance and/or an emotional reaction to being told what to do. Place yourself in their position. Would you rather be told to do something or would you rather be asked to do something? When possible, officials should be asking rather than telling the coaches and players what to do (Maxim #2). People are listening (someone may be recording the game) to what you are saying. By asking you show them respect.

Here is an example. The players on the bench during a basketball game are complaining to the officials about fouls not being called.

As the official runs by the bench, he says to the coach, "Keep your bench quiet, I'm not going to listen to that." Or the official stops play and begins to lecture the bench in front of the crowd. Remember what our goal is here? It's the 3 C's. Do you think that there is a chance that this official will be able to generate compliance, cooperation and collaboration with players, coaches and the fans? The answer is probably not.

The better tactic for the official is to appeal to the coach. How about this response from the official: "Coach, help me out here and ask your players to stop complaining about the calls." Find your personal comfort zone in how to rephrase your statement into a question that defuses anger and builds engagement. Use professional language that moves toward generating the 3 C's.

A second example is referred to as Good Speak. Good Speak is the professional use of words used to achieve a professional objective. It puts the official in contact with the players and coaches through the use of skillful communications that is right on target with the audience. The opposite is Bad Speak, which is unprofessional language. The official starts to express his or her personal feelings by using self-referential words such as "I" and "me". It is not all about you; it is about the game. By using self-referential language you are not in contact with the players and coaches and you start generating resistance from the audience. That will make this a long game.

Officials do not need to explain the reason they make every call. Explanations can interrupt the flow of a game. But there are times when an official can and should give an explanation to a player and/

or coach (Maxim #3). Remember the first Great American Question: Why? Explaining why you ask someone to do something or why you made that decision or call shows respect.

My father coached basketball on the grade school, high school and college level for over 40 years. He was well respected by his peers, players and officials. He was inducted into the Wisconsin Basketball Coach's Hall of Fame in 2003. Dad had a ridiculously low number of technical fouls (2 or 3) for someone who coached that long. I attended one of his high school games toward the end of his coaching career. One of his players received a technical foul during the game. My dad asked the official what the players had said or done. The official's response was to walk away from dad. He followed the official onto the floor requesting an explanation and was subsequently given a technical foul. By walking away the official was sending the message "I don't have to tell you anything and I don't respect you." An explanation was warranted in this situation. I once asked my dad the reason for his technical fouls. He said it was because of his frustration with officials that showed arrogance by not taking the time to answer questions. The first Great American Question is "Why". Take the time to answer the questions when you can. That simple courtesy will begin to generate respect.

There are times that an explanation may not be enough to sway a player or coach. The resistance continues but the official needs to resume the game. If the player or coach's behavior hasn't reached the level of an ejection or some type of sanction, then give them some options rather than threatening them with an ejection (Maxim #4). This leaves them in control of their own situation. It allows them to save face and reduces the chance of them continuing to posture. Threatening people reduces your options and backs you into a corner. Giving them options provides a "wake up call" for the player or coach. It brings them back to reality by saying "Coach, I explained why I made the call and I'm not going to change it. This is a good game, so let's end this conversation and get the game going. Otherwise I will have to eject you. Work with me here so we can continue the game."

Here's what that means in the officials' head: "I made the call. I understand you are upset. I showed you respect by explaining the call. You needed more time to process the information so I gave you some options you could choose from. What else would you like me to do?"

Maxim #5 says, "Give people a second chance." So when it is possible, give them that second chance. There is a great deal of emotion involved in athletics and it's not going away. As long as that emotion doesn't result in a level of conduct that needs to be sanctioned, then deal with it appropriately. I have attended many football, baseball, softball and basketball games. A call is made by an official or umpire, and noises erupt from the crowd - the "oohs," "ah's" and "come-ons" that come from the players, coaches and fans. Sometimes an official or umpire overreacts and starts threatening whoever said something. What do officials expect to happen in these instances? Applause from the crowd? Someone yelling "great call?"

That's not going to happen (unless the call benefited their team). Also, the younger the player is, the more reaction you may get. Like the 10-year-old kid that throws his bat on the ground after striking out with the bases loaded. Will ejecting him in front of the crowd be a teaching moment or a devastating moment of great embarrassment? Wouldn't it be better to talk to the coach so he or she can explain to the player how to handle failure? The same is true for newer coaches. New coaches are learning how to coach and how to behave during the game. I believe officials have a part to play in the education of new coaches. That means that we as officials should model proper behavior on the field. You can show them the way by maintaining your emotional equilibrium.

By giving people a second chance you are sending them a message that says, "I understand you are not happy with that call (or no call). You can have a reaction as long as it does not reach a level that conveys unsportsmanlike conduct during the game". The alternative is having complete silence with no one being able to say anything during the game. That would include players, coaches and spectators. Is that what we really want?

In concluding this section on the Five Maxims of Communications, I would like to share this story. In 2004 I had the privilege of umpiring in a state championship high school baseball tournament. I was the home plate umpire in a quarterfinal game. The tournament was played in a minor league ballpark in which the stands were full with about two thousand spectators. The game started with the team (Team A) that was an "underdog" leading the team (Team B) that was expected to win (and did win) their division in the tournament. After a rain delay in the 4th inning, the wheels began to fall off of the wagon for Team A. In other words, they had committed a few errors and were now losing the game. Team A was on defense when a player from Team B stole second base. It was close, and the second base umpire called him safe (the right call). Team A's catcher walked out in front of home plate and threw his glove on the ground in response to the outcome. He walked toward the pitcher's mound. I followed him and at the same time Team A's coach called time out.

Do I eject the catcher or talk to him? The coach began to walk toward the pitcher's mound. My intent was to talk to the catcher about his actions. The coach said to me, "Pete, I'll handle this and talk to him." I told him okay and thanks, and walked to the third base line as Team A's coach had a meeting on the pitcher's mound. Team B's coach came down the line and wanted to know why I didn't eject the catcher. I explained why and then asked him to return to the coach's box. After the inning was over the coach from Team A came out to talk to me. He thanked me for allowing him to calm his catcher down. He added that the catcher was a student with a learning disability and that he really appreciated the fact that I didn't eject him. What would have been accomplished by ejecting the catcher, in front of two thousand people, for an emotional outburst? They lost the game; it was his last game. That would have been his last memory of playing baseball in the state championship. Yes, the behavior needed to be addressed and it was. Sometimes it's better for us as officials to disappear and let the coaches handle the kids.

Chapter 2 Learning Points

- **Everyone wants to be treated with dignity and everyone wants to be shown respect.** It doesn't matter what environment you are in. You could be at the grocery store, at work, coaching in a basketball game or officiating a game. The Five

Maxims of Communications are the foundation for building this respect. Once you internalize these maxims you will be well on your way to understanding the tactics that are discussed in this book. The "Five Maxims" are the philosophy that drives the Verbal Defense & Influence tactics.

- **Listening to people is not just hearing what they say.** You must utilize all of your senses to gather as much information from that person as possible. Listen to everything happening during the game, not just to a single person. Listen to and see what is happening on the court, field, or bench areas. This allows you make a more thorough assessment of how the game is going. The information you gather aids you in preparing to handle the inevitable conflict.
- **The maturity levels of the players and coaches vary depending on what level you are officiating.** In other words, the new coaches and players on the youth levels need to mature. The younger the athlete, the less mature s/he is. The newer the coach, the less mature s/he is in understanding how to appropriately behave during the game. Therefore it is important "to give someone a second chance" to understand how to act when they feel they have been wronged. It is your opportunity to model proper behavior during the conflict.

Chapter 3

Showtime (Get Yourself Ready To Manage The Game)

John the umpire is assigned to work multiple games in a high school "wood bat" baseball tournament on a Saturday. The games are being played at two different sites. The championship game is set for 5:00 pm but is delayed because the game at the other site went into extra innings. It's now 6:00 pm and the teams are ready to start. The coaches meet at home plate for ground rules. John announces that he doesn't want to be there and that he has a wedding to go to tonight. Is John in the right mindset to umpire that game? Should John be saying that at ground rules? How much personal baggage has John dragged onto the field? If John makes a bad call, how much grief do you think he is going to get? This happens more than it should in any sport. Officials bring their personal baggage to the field and aren't ready to officiate.

Sports officials come in all shapes and sizes. They work in various professions. Many people officiate in more than one sport. In my case, I worked in law enforcement full-time for 25 years. I also worked as a firefighter part-time for the past 33 years. I officiated one sport, baseball, often leaving work and going to the field to umpire a game. I umpired on many of my Saturdays off, and worked in a profession that is described as stressful. So it was important to me to not bring that stress to the field. When I walked onto the field, I was no longer Pete the deputy sheriff (or firefighter), instead becoming Pete the umpire. Umpiring baseball became my stress relief. How can people leave that stress at home, work or any other place so they can enjoy the experience of officiating? The answer is to develop a mindset that says, "It's Showtime".

There are two types of faces that people present when they talk to other people. We call these faces the Professional Face and the Personal Face. The Professional Face is the face we put on to match whatever task is in front of us. It may be our law enforcement face, attorney face, doctor face or accountant face. The Personal Face is one we share with those we have close relationships with. This may be your family and friends.

Showtime is a tactic that prepares you to put on that Professional Face. The Professional Face allows you to deal with the task at hand, officiating an athletic event. But there are other tasks that occur during the event. These can include pre-game meetings with the coaches, making a call or handling a dispute. Each task may require a different Professional Face. You essentially become a chameleon that is able to change colors to adapt to its environment. The only difference is that you are changing your face to adapt to the task that is front of you.

The Professional Face is very important in terms of how people view you as an official. Are you viewed as too aggressive, too weak, too young, or too old? Or are you just right (assertive, knowledgeable, and competent)? Think of this analogy. When two people meet there are really six people in the room. Here are those six people:

First there is you:

- Real self - who you really are
- Self as seen by self - who you think you are
- Self as seen by others - how people view you

Then there is the person you are talking to:

- Real self - who s/he really is
- Self as seen by self - who s/he thinks s/he is
- Self as seen by others - how you view him or her

At an athletic event you can add even more "people". When you add the coaches, players and the crowd, you have a lot of "selves" out there. As an official, how people view you is the most important for you. If they view you as fair, unbiased, competent and open, you are more likely to gain that compliance, cooperation or collaboration from the players and coaches (and the fans). You can accomplish this by presenting your Professional Face.

So why is Showtime a benefit for officials? The answer is that it enhances your professionalism. It prepares you mentally for the task at hand. It reminds you to use your Professional Face and professional words when you officiate. Sports officials have to detach themselves from the emotions of the game. They have to maintain an emotional equilibrium. They should be unbiased when they make calls or decisions, flexible when they deal with conflict and open in their communications with the players and coaches.

Showtime is a tactic that can be learned through practice. So let's breakdown how you perform the tactic of 'Showtime'':

1. Stack up your blocks
2. Say "Showtime" to yourself
3. Breathe in, pause, breathe out, pause and repeat (each is usually a four second count)
4. Put on your Professional Face
5. Use the appropriate positive self-talk
6. Step into the arena and handle it

Let's break each section down. Andrew Garrison, a wellness expert and consultant within Vistelar, describes "Stacking Your Blocks" as a postural technique. It starts from the ground up and creates the proper physiological position for you. It also raises your testosterone levels and reduces cortisol levels (which is a stress hormone). The importance of posturing has been highlighted in an Association for Psychological Science Research Report (2010) titled, "Power Posing: Brief Nonverbal Displays Affect Neuroendocrine Levels and Risk Tolerance." The study supports the claim that posture can increase testosterone levels while decreasing the stress hormone cortisol.

How to "Stack your Blocks":

- Ground your feet 4-6 inches apart- Drive them into the ground
- Relax your knees (bend slightly)
- Pelvis- tuck in your buttocks and drive your naval through your thoracic vertebrae (back)
- Take in a deep breath to raise your rib cage off of your pelvis and to drive your scapula down

- Andrew Garrison

The second step in Showtime is simply telling yourself, it's "Showtime." If I make a call on a close play in a baseball game, I expect some sort of reaction. If the coach comes out to challenge the call, I get in the proper stance (Stacking Up My Blocks) and say to myself "here he comes, it's Showtime." I then begin to "autogenic breathe." The process is to breathe in through your nose for four seconds and then out through your mouth for four seconds, pause and then continue the same process. If I don't have the time to complete the process, I shorten the breath (when the coach leaves the field I continue to breathe). I then put on my Professional Face and say to myself "I've got this." I'm now ready to step into the arena and talk to the coach.

I also utilize the Showtime tactic to prepare for the game. Officials usually meet before the game to discuss how the contest will be officiated (pre-game meetings). You can and should go through the Showtime process while getting dressed and going through the pregame with your partner(s).

Bill Dittmar, who I referenced earlier, told a story in Ellensburg, Washington, as we were training soccer officials. He was an assistant referee (sideline) in a Major League Soccer game when he made an offside call at a critical point in the game. He was sure he had the call right. Bill told me that his wife Heidi watches his games on television. When he spoke to her after the game she asked him if he was sure he made the right call on that play. He asked "why?" She stated that he didn't look "confident" in making the call because of his facial expression, which was shown on TV. What she was referring to was that while he was raising his flag to make the signal, the camera caught him licking sweat off his upper lip. When Bill later saw a replay of the game, he agreed with his wife that that simple gesture did make him look less confident in his call. He told me it was hot and humid that day. This was caught on camera. It wasn't the face Bill wanted the viewers to see. It didn't show the confidence in the call that he really had. It wasn't his "Showtime" face. The learning point here is that there is no dark alley to hide in anymore. We have to look good and look confident when we make our calls.

There is one final point on "Showtime." The majority of people who officiate a sport wear a uniform. The uniform identifies you as an official. There are spectators at the event who watch the athletes and you. You probably are being recorded on somebody's camera or phone. You are essentially on a stage. Your role is that of the Official. So you need to look good, sound good and be good at officiating. Did you look in the mirror or check your uniform before you put it on? Are there any stains on your shirt? Are your pants wrinkled? Did you shave? What kind of physical shape are you in? Take the time to look good and prepare yourself mentally to officiate the event. It only helps you.

Chapter 3 Learning Points

- **Almost everyone that officiates a sport has another job or is a student.** These other occupations can put you into a mindset that may not be conducive to officiating a baseball, basketball, volleyball or soccer game. Some jobs we work can also be stressful. Therefore you must prepare yourself mentally to enter that arena to officiate a game. This will eliminate any biases that you may bring to the event that would hinder your performance efficiency. Showtime mentally prepares you to officiate that game.
- **There are two faces you can present when you are officiating.** The first is the Professional Face. This is the face you want on the court or field. It is the face that allows you to handle the task that is at hand. The second face is the Personal Face. This is the face you show to your family and friends. Showtime is a tactic that prepares you to use your Professional Face.
- **How people view you is important in terms of how you will be able to generate voluntary compliance, cooperation or collaboration during the game.** You need to look good, sound good and be good to be successful. Showtime enhances your professionalism.
- **"Stacking up your blocks" is a postural technique that reduces your stress level.** When you are under stress your pulse rate increases, your palms become sweaty and you reduce oxygen

intake to your brain. By "stacking up your blocks" and completing the steps in the Showtime tactic, you regain control of these physiological reactions, bringing them under control. This allows you to perform efficiently under stressful conditions.

Chapter 4

Universal Greeting (Set The Stage For Collaboration)

It's a beautiful sunny day in July. John and his partner Jim are umpiring a 14-year-old youth baseball tournament. Jim is the plate umpire and John will umpire the bases. They both get to the ballpark 45 minutes before game time. They conduct their pre-game meeting with each other and get dressed (they look good). It's now time to head to the field for the ground rules (meeting with coaches and captains). They get to home plate and Jim opens up the conversation by stating, "Here's how I'm going to run this game." He continues by explaining his strike zone and that he won't tolerate any disagreements during the game. He uses the word "I" ten times during the meeting, referring to how "he" will umpire the game. What kind of impression do you think the players and coaches have of Jim (and his partner John)? Has Jim created a supportive or defensive atmosphere for the players and coaches during game? Has Jim made it easy for him and his partner to get compliance, cooperation and/or collaboration during the game? The answer is "probably not."

Meetings like this occur in all sports. There is always a point when the officials make their initial contact with the players and coaches (at all levels of sports). Many people are watching to see who that official(s) is/are way before the game starts. Once they see you, they begin forming an impression based on how you come across. In Malcolm Gladwell's book, "Blink: The Power of Thinking Without Thinking," he examines the process he calls thin-slicing in which people formulate an impression of you within two seconds. The players, coaches and fans thin-slice officials and officials do their own thin-slicing. In general, the impact of thin-slicing is felt in the building of relationships and how people interact with each other (agreements and disagreements). Therefore, how you make an initial contact with someone is very important. It is setting the stage for how you manage the game. The VDI tactic for this is the Universal Greeting:

1. Give an appropriate greeting. This shows respect and is professional and pleasant.
2. Introduce yourself (if they haven't met you before) and your role as an official (if they don't know Umpire, Crew Chief, Line Judge, and Side Line Official, etc.). This answers the Great American Questions of "Who are you?" and "Where do you get your authority?"
3. Explain your reason for initiating the contact (Great American Question # 1, "Why?"). Is it ground rules, equipment inspection, pre-game meeting? Every sport has its own procedures, just explain yourself.

4. Ask a relevant question (Maxim #2, "Ask, don't tell"). "Can I see your line-up cards? Please line up so we can check your shin guards. Can we see your bats and helmets? Is everyone properly equipped?" These are examples of questions you may have.

The pre-game meetings or ground rules also allow you to set the "Social Contract" for the game. This concept was created by Joel Lashley, a Training Consultant for Vistelar. The Merriam-Webster definition of Social Contract is as follows: "an actual or hypothetical agreement among the members of an organized society or between a community and its ruler that defines and limits the rights and duties of each." I think of it as those rules in sport that may not necessarily be written, such as not stealing bases when you are winning by 15 runs or throwing passes down field when you are winning by 4 touchdowns in the last 3 minutes of a game. This doesn't mean you need to talk about all of these things during your meetings. You run the risk of being too long winded and giving the impression that you are a dictator and not an official. Officials may mention things, such as how to approach them if you want to discuss a call, or they mention the need for sportsmanship during the game. In some sports and organizations there are certain requirements for reminding the coaches and players that they have to behave. The pre-game meeting is your opportunity to set the social contract for how the game will be managed.

In my experiences, "behavior" is a relative term for some people. In my ground rules, I remind coaches that I would rather they come to talk to me instead of yelling at me from the dugout or from 90 feet away. It's hard to accomplish anything from that distance (except maybe an ejection). The pre-game meetings are your opportunity to set the Social Contract when it comes to discussing calls and sportsmanship. One caution is that you shouldn't be using the "I" word too much when you talk about these things. That puts too much focus on you.

There are benefits to initially greeting people properly. This assists you in managing conflict that may occur later in the event. The Universal Greeting is professional and pleasant, which helps to overcome any of the players' or coaches' negative perceptions of you as an official (or perceptions you have of a coach). These perceptions could be the result of a previous encounter with a coach or they could be the negative perceptions players and coaches have of officials (it happens at all levels). You want to show the players and coaches that you are not a "jerk." I once had a rough encounter with a high school coach in a state tournament. There were several conflicts that occurred in two games during that tournament. The following season I umpired a regional tournament game involving the same team and coach. I made it a point to be spot on with the Universal Greeting when we met at ground rules. It went great. The meeting was pleasant and professional; we even talked about the tournament from last year. This reduced the tensions and led to a more pleasant experience for both of us during the game.

The Universal Greeting also allows you to "test the waters" during the pre-game meetings. You get a sense of how the coaches and teams are feeling today. If you go into the meeting overly aggressive (you don't let anyone talk), you will get little information that would have allowed you to head off and handle any conflicts that may have occurred during the game. There are clues sent out by the coaches that will let you know if there will be friction between the teams, players, coaches or officials. How the participants at the meeting interact with each other may give you some clues. If you are professional and pleasant, then you can eliminate yourself as the antagonist. The information you gain at the pre-game meeting may lead to some good intelligence for you. That intelligence may well help you later in the game when dealing with conflict.

Vistelar and its training consultants are always receiving requests for training courses that center around de-escalation tactics. In other words, how as officials do we communicate with the players and coaches when they are losing it on the field? Officials sometimes do things that set people off. In many instances, we don't even know we are doing this. Yet in some instances there are officials who bait people into bad behavior. In either case, we call this the P.O.P index. This stands for how to "Provoke Other People."

The importance of the "P.O.P. Index" can't be overstated. That's because 93% of your success in communicating is based on your delivery style. This includes both your physical actions and your speech. The physical is as follows:

- Facial expressions can convey disinterest, disgust, anger and annoyance.
- Your attitude may convey superiority; you may be argumentative or dismissive.
- You may display mannerisms that convey being inapproachable.

Such as the use of the "hand" to stop someone from talking.

The speech that provokes people is as follows:

- The use of profanity.
- The use of "buzzwords." Buzzwords are trending words and phrases that are usually negative. They can be ethnic slurs, racial slurs or any other kinds of slurs.
- The use of a "verbal parting shot." We don't always have to have the last word. Remember that if it felt good for you to say it, it probably wasn't the right thing to say.

As an athletic official, you may be officiating sports on the youth level. This means you could have players and coaches with little or no experience in competitive sports. So where do they learn how to interact with the officials? The coaches may have personal experience from when they participated in a sport. The kids may get it from watching games on television or in person, or from watching movies that deal with sports. The experiences these people have may be good experiences or they may be bad experiences. Either way you have an opportunity to mold their experiences with officials by modeling proper behavior during the game. I stress this when speaking to umpires at the youth level. You have an effect on the development of those players and coaches. I have even encountered coaches at the high school level that need to be shown proper behavior on the field. The Universal Greeting helps in that modeling process.

The final benefit to the Universal Greeting is that it makes you look good no matter how the game or event goes. You can make a great call and still have conflict. The coach or player may still feel the call was wrong. That can happen any time. When they question the call, you want that discussion to be professional, and the chances are good it will be because of the supportive atmosphere you created during the pre-game meeting. But the coach's behavior may escalate to a point that you have to eject him (even though you handled it professionally).

A parent has been videotaping you and the coach. The good news is that it was the coach that looked bad on the video. But what if you didn't set up that supportive atmosphere, because you handled the pre-game meeting and/or the conflict unprofessionally (you lost control)? Instead of you looking good on the video, you came off as the aggressor. The video was uploaded to social media and it was titled "official loses control." It got thousands of hits. But how can this be happening? You made the right call or decision. Nobody watching the game or video remembers your great call because you colored your good call with your unacceptable behavior. The focus is now on your behavior because you are the person who has the authority. This is why you want to look good no matter where the situation ends up.

Let's talk about the challenges that different age groups and genders face when officiating and how the Universal Greeting can help to cultivate respect between the players, coaches and officials. About one half of my umpire trainees are teenagers I have also trained female umpires (softball and baseball). Every sport has their share of young officials and female officials. The relationship between the adult coach and youth official can be intimidating for the youth official, as can the relationship between males and females. Your credibility is being examined during the pre-game meeting, so the

Universal Greeting becomes important. You do not want to give a perception to the players and coaches of being passive or meek. Conversely you don't want to be pushy or aggressive. You want to be assertive. This gives them an impression that you are firm, but fair. By following the steps to the Universal Greeting and scripting out and practicing your pre-game meetings you convey competence and assertiveness. I make my umpire trainees perform the Universal Greetings in their training. I use "ground rules" as the simulation.

All officials should have a script for their pre-game meetings, regardless of your age or gender. There are officials who are "bully magnets" that are easily manipulated by coaches and players. There are also officials that portray themselves as pushy or overly aggressive. To project assertiveness and competence you should take the time to practice your scripts.

Here's how I conduct my ground rule (pre-game) meeting. First, I stand facing the field (my partner(s) stand facing me). The coaches are to my left and right. If we have not met the coaches, we introduce ourselves (there may be players at the ground rules so we introduce ourselves to the players). They all know that they are there for ground rules so I move on to asking a relevant question(s) such as, "Can I have your line-up cards?" Other questions are asked such as, "Are your players properly equipped?" Finally, I ask the home field coach to "take us around the field" and give us the ground rules for their field. I then conclude the meeting by asking if there are any other questions and I state, "Have a good game." This is my script for how I conduct "ground rules." Other officials may say and do it differently. That's okay as long as it is professional and sets the tone for generating compliance, cooperation and/or collaboration during the game. Create your script and practice it.

Chapter 4 Learning Points

- **First impressions are important in terms of how people view you.** The players, coaches and fans "thin slice" you during the pre-game meetings. By using a scripted and practiced Universal Greeting, you are being professional and pleasant. It also allows you to overcome any adversarial relationships that may be present before the game even starts.
- **Every sport has the time when the coaches and players first meet.** This is the time to show the coaches and players that you are not a "jerk." You can set the rules (Social Contract) on how you want to handle the situations that involve conflict. Be careful not to use self-referential language such as the word "I." When you begin sentences with the word "I," you run the risk of portraying yourself as being too aggressive. Remember that you are not the show. You want to disappear during the game, while at the same time being able to manage the game effectively.
- **By being professional and pleasant you can test the waters to see how the players and coaches are feeling today.** There is information that can be gained by observing how they interact with you and each other during the pre-game meetings. You can see things such as the tensions between the teams, the coaches or maybe how they feel towards you and your partner.

- **As officials we need to be aware of the fact that there are things that we may do that provoke other people (P.O.P Index).** We may not even know that we are doing these things. That's why it so important to script out and practice a proper Universal Greeting. You can than eliminate the potential of doing or saying something wrong which may provoke a coach or player before the game even begins.
- **There are challenges faced by young officials and female officials that may be officiating in a male dominated sport.** The use of the Showtime tactic and a proper Universal Greeting can project assertiveness, confidence and credibility. Don't become a "bully magnet" that can be manipulated by the players and coaches.

Chapter 5

Beyond Active Listening (Pay Attention So You Can Respond)

It's hard for anyone to listen to a person who is yelling at them. It's even harder for the person in authority to listen to someone who is yelling at them. Let me ask you this question: "What is the opposite of talking?" The answer should be "listening." But is that what we really do when someone is yelling at us? No, we aren't listening. We wait to interrupt them so we can say what we have to say, especially if we know and/or think we are right. The challenge for us is to learn how to listen to people so we can effectively communicate with them when they think they have been wronged and they go into crisis mode.

I just referred to players, coaches and fans as going into a crisis mode. Let's define the word crisis to better understand why players, coaches and fans become emotional during an athletic event. The Webster definition is as follows: *a difficult or dangerous situation that needs serious attention.* Is being on the wrong end of a decision or call in a game a crisis? For athletes and coaches it can be. For others they say something like, "It's just a game." If you really want to set off a competitive person say, "It's just a game." I like to think of the word "crisis" in this way: A law enforcement colleague of mine once made this statement, "It was a crisis in their minds." I like this statement because it tells me that everyone defines their own crisis (a difficult situation that they feel needs serious attention). Don't coaches and players experience their own crisis during the event? Yes they do. That's why they get upset. We need to listen to them so we can determine what their crisis really is. Then we can address the issue that put them into the crisis.

Earlier I wrote about Bill Dittmar's drill called "sounds of the game." This drill was designed to teach soccer officials how to be aware of everything that goes on during the game. You also have to utilize your other senses. There are things happening during the game or event that need our attention or at least we need to know that they are happening. We may hear things that are said to us or said between players, coaches and the teams. We may also see things that may indicate a problem, things such as physical contact between players, or gestures made between players and coaches. Listening becomes an exercise using other senses than just your hearing.

Let's take a look at this scenario in a basketball game. You are officiating a high school game between two rivals that have similar records in their conference. This is a "big game" to them. I use this term "big game" facetiously. My umpire partners and I always joke about this term when we hear it from coaches and players in this context: "How can you make a call like that in such a "big game."

If it wasn't a "big game," should we make a different call? I don't think that's our goal as officials. The coaches and players will also use the term to explain away their bad behavior just because it is a "big game." Does that mean that we officiate differently in "big games?" The answer would be no, we can't officiate a game differently just because it is a "big game." The point here is that people's perceptions can affect their behavior and we need to understand that. All that hype can lead to tension during the game. As officials we need to maintain our emotional equilibrium so we can see and hear the "sounds of the game." Then we can manage it more effectively.

During the early minutes of a basketball game there are a few hard screens and fouls. The coaches start saying things to each other across the benches. You and your partners see and hear this. What do you do? Let it go and think to yourself: "Wow, this is going to be a rough game," or are you going to address it? This is a hard concept to teach to officials. When should you intervene? If you remember that the earlier you intervene the less trouble will occur later in the game it will help you keep order. It doesn't matter what sport you officiate. Tension between players and coaches can happen in any sport. The longer it continues, the greater the chance that something physical is going to happen. Joel Lashley refers to this as "gateway behaviors." These are the little things that happen early in the game. If we don't address the behaviors early, they will continue to mount. They may get to a point where the game gets too physical. At this point the damage is done and you may have lost control of the game. You should address the "gateway behaviors" when they happen. That's why you have to remember to remain alert (listen with all of your senses), make a decision (intervene now) and have a pre-planned, practiced response to deal with the issue.

In order for an official to respond to a coach or player, they have to listen. Listening is a skill. It's a skill that we need to improve. This is especially true when you are trying to listen to someone who is excited, emotional and maybe out of control. You can gain so much information from listening appropriately. You can then formulate a response that corresponds to what is really bothering the coach or player.

Listening involves the following components:

- You have to be unbiased, flexible and open;
- You have to listen, literally, to what is being said (don't just watch their lips move);
- You have to accurately interpret what is being said;
- You have to act appropriately to what is being said.

All officials need to be unbiased. That's a major ethical part of officiating. But can we be biased without even realizing it? Sure, it happens. It happens when you start having discussions about player and coach behavior before the start of the game. "I had these guys last week. They whine about every call." My response would be: "Really? Were they right?" By starting the game with a pre-conceived notion that they "whine," you are pre-loading yourself to be biased. Yes, we do discuss the behavior of coaches and players. And their behavior at times may be over the top. But we need to be transparent about what caused the behavior. The only way to know what caused the behavior is to be unbiased and listen.

Listening also conveys flexibility and openness. If you don't listen, you convey rigidity and you lose contact with the players and coaches. Without that contact, you have less of a chance of gaining compliance, cooperation and/or collaboration with anybody associated with the game.

There are a lot of things that are said by coaches and players during the game. It is important for officials to hear literally what is said so they can act appropriately. Sometimes the best action is no action. It may be appropriate to just let it go.

Listening also includes several other components that are important for your success in communicating with the players and coaches. Pay attention to the words being used. There are cues in these words that will give you an understanding of why they are upset and what may happen next. Some words indicate that there may be physical contact about to occur, and in some cases an assault could be coming your way. The tone of voice also plays an important role in understanding the mindset of the person you are listening to. Is it soft (calmness) or is it loud (frustration/anger)? Pay attention to the person's facial expression. Does the face indicate anger through tension, frustration or maybe confusion? Is their body language indicating openness, anger through tension or do they flail around, which can indicate frustration and anger? Again, body language can indicate physical contact or an assault is about to occur. It's something that sports officials must pay attention to.

The context of the situation also needs to be assessed. Are they upset about something that makes no sense at all? In other words, have you made a ruling or call that's a "no brainer" and they are out there to make a point about something else? I like it when officials talk about coaches that enjoy "working the officials" so they can get a call in their favor. That raises my antenna and amuses me.

When I first began umpiring on the college level, I was tested in a NCAA Division III baseball game. I was umpiring behind the plate and called a few balls on pitches that I saw as low. It was borderline on whether they were a strike or a ball but I was comfortable with calling them balls. I heard this several times from the dugout: "We need that pitch, we teach them to throw that pitch down there." My answer was: "Teach them to throw it higher." That felt good when I said it, so it was probably not the right thing to say. This was before I had understood the value of VDI. Today my response would have been, "I got that coach, but I have it down in the zone. He needs to bring that pitch up." We'll talk about that later when we discuss Redirections. The coach saw me as a new umpire and was testing me. After the game, he walked by my partner and me and stated, "You did alright."

The final component to listening is to consider the distance the person is from you and the position you are in. Are they talking or yelling from the bench, did they sprint on to the field/court and get into your face? Are you able to position yourself with your back to the benches and crowd (no one else needs to hear what is being said)? Are you able to control the distance and positioning? If not, is it because they keep moving closer or laterally to the left or right? This is an indicator that there is no communicating taking place. The more uncontrolled movement that occurs hinders the ability to communicate. This is the time to act (technical foul, ejection, flag, and any other appropriate sanction).

Let's talk about "empathy." This is the most important quality for an official to have when dealing with people that are in crisis. Empathy is mentally putting yourself into another person's circumstances to experience it through his or her eyes. Let me share this story with you to explain the importance of empathy.

I was umpiring a high school baseball game between two very good programs with very good coaches. I was the home plate umpire. My partner for this game was a good friend and a good experienced umpire, Dan Deremer. During ground rules, the coaches discussed how their seasons had been going up to that point in the season. The coach from "Team A" expressed his frustration with his team's inability to score runs.

During the top half of the 5th inning, "Team A" was winning 2 to 1. "Team A" was at bat and had runners on first and second base with one out in the inning. A right-handed hitter from "Team A" hit a hard line drive down the right field line. The ball was tailing slightly toward the right field foul line. The right fielder took a path toward the ball that placed him right on top of the foul line running out toward the right field fence, blocking my view of the foul line. My responsibility on this type of play was to rule fair or foul and to cover home plate. Therefore I took a few steps in front of home plate, on top of the foul line between home and first base. Here's what I was thinking: "Crap, I can't see the foul line!" I had a 50% chance of getting it right based on my judgment of where the ball might hit.

The ball, which was tailing slightly, hit the ground and instantly bounced over the right field fence. I immediately put my hands up and emphatically called "foul." The right fielder, at the same time I called foul, held his hands up indicating that the ball bounced over the fence for a ground rule double. In other words, I called a foul ball and the right fielder told everyone it bounced over the fence, fair.

Has this ever happened to you? I instantly felt my stomach drop. I was overwhelmed with a feeling of indecision. Time stopped in my mind. I thought, "Oh my God. Did I just kick this call?" The coach from "Team A" came down the third baseline from the coach's box and began to express his displeasure with my call. I met him up the third base line and thought: "I would be doing the same thing you are doing." That's empathy! He did not say or do anything that warranted an ejection. I just let him go for about 30 seconds, and then said the following: "Ernie, can I tell you what happened? I couldn't see the foul line because the right fielder was right on the line. I made an educated guess based on the trajectory of the ball. I know how you feel and I'd be out here too if I was in your shoes. But there's nothing I can do to change the call (I can't go by the fact that the right fielder did what he did so the ball must have been fair)."

The coach began listening to me. He was standing, looking at the ground with his hat in his hand. He said a few more things trying to figure out what just happened and then he returned to the coach's box. I went behind home plate and I thought: "Please God, let this kid get a hit." He didn't get a hit and the inning ended with "Team A" not scoring a run. My foul ball call cost them at least one run in a 2 to 1 game.

The inning ended and the coach came by me as he entered his dugout and said, "That was such a big call, couldn't you have asked your partner?" The answer to that was no, Dan was in no position to see the ball hit the ground either foul or fair. As I was cleaning off home plate to begin the bottom half of the inning, the coach from Team A came out of the dugout and said to me: "Pete, I have a parent who was sitting on the right field foul line. He said the ball was clearly foul." I got it right! I looked up from a bent over position and said: "Thanks Ernie, you have a lot of class."

First of all, this story could and probably has happened to other umpires. There are other umpires that probably would have handled it like I did. The teaching points here are important. There was a lot of respect that was exhibited on that field, a respect that was cultivated through previous interactions with these coaches.

My empathy was genuine and it showed him respect. He returned the respect by listening to me and by telling me I had gotten the call right. This could have gone really bad. I could have been rigid and not listened to him when he came out to argue. I know some umpires that may have told him to go back to the coach's box. This could have made the situation worse, which may have caused the coach to escalate his behavior, which may have led to an ejection. By the way, the game ended with "Team A" winning 2 to 1.

By utilizing the skills of listening and mastering the tactic of empathy, you are well on your way to managing your communication with the players and coaches. By listening you are gaining intelligence on where the players and coaches are at that moment. You can use that intelligence to gain compliance, cooperation or collaboration.

By exercising empathy you find out where they have been in the past. You are seeing the situation through their eyes. The past means earlier in the game and in their previous games. When you combine listening and empathy, you can predict where they may be later in the game. You are constructing a verbal means so you can relate to the players and coaches. Empathy doesn't mean agreeing with them. It means you are simply trying to understand their perspective.

For example, there are games played in which calls may seem to be going the wrong way for a particular team. The perception is that the officials are not consistent with their calls -- too many fouls in a basketball game, too many walks in a baseball game or too many fouls called in a soccer game. The coach or players become upset over a particular call (even though the call was correct). You explain your reason for the call and the games goes on. You listened and you heard what they said. You show empathy by understanding why they may be upset. You can almost predict what's going to happen on the next close or controversial call. Remember that in order to communicate properly you want to respond and not react. Being able to predict what is going to happen when you make a call allows you to plan your response. When you have a pre-planned response, you look and sound good.

There are times when you may need to ask questions when you talk to a coach or player who is upset. There are several types of questions that can be asked. They range from fact-finding questions, opinion-seeking questions and leading questions that are all not generally applicable in the situations that occur in sports. The questions that officials may ask are either general or direct questions. I find that in most instances, officials ask questions to clarify what players and coaches are saying. Questions such as, "Coach, what did you see on that call?" A question like this allows you to understand why the coach came out and it helps you to formulate a response that addresses the reason they are questioning a call. There are times when people in crisis say things that they don't mean. Words fly out of their mouth but the real meaning lags behind. We have to clarify what their meaning is by asking questions. Therefore, another type of question would be, "So coach, you came out here because you thought he missed the tag?" They may modify their answer. Now you have the right reason that they came out to argue the call.

I have talked about listening and how important it is to show respect to the players and coaches (as long as it doesn't reach the level of inappropriate words and behavior). The question I am often asked by new officials is: "How much do you listen?" "When is it time for the officials to talk? You can't stand there all game and wait for them to stop talking."

The best way to interrupt a player or coach appropriately is to paraphrase what they are saying to you. The VDI program refers to this as the sword of insertion. You are putting what you perceive to be the meaning of their words into your words. You can then both understand what is being said. If you misinterpret what they were saying, they may well modify what they are trying to say to you. Now you will have the right message so you can respond appropriately.

Paraphrasing also allows you to interrupt without generating resistance from the player or coach you are talking to. Once you repeat what they are saying back to them they will begin to listen to you.

This happens because no one will listen harder than to their own point-of-view. This also creates empathy. They will begin to believe that you are trying to understand what made them upset.

Here is an example of using a paraphrase to interrupt. "Coach, let me try and understand what you are saying." Now you can follow-up with their perceived meaning in your words. "You are saying that you think he traveled before the foul was committed?" The coach can now affirm what you said or he or she can modify their statement. In any case, you have begun to create empathy and have shown respect by listening.

The final component of Beyond Active Listening is to summarize your calls or decisions when it is appropriate. Summarizing creates decisiveness and reinforces your authority as an official. You don't lose authority when you communicate during the game. Just don't wear your authority on your forehead by being overly aggressive. It also helps to reconnect communication if for some reason there is a temporary interruption in the discussion. You also want to make sure everyone involved in the discussion understands the outcome. This will help you later when reports need to be written or there are inquiries from other people who have regulating authority over your sport (suspensions, protests or other issues).

Chapter 5 Learning Points

- **The opposite of talking should be listening.** But for people who have a point to make in a discussion, the opposite of talking becomes "waiting to interrupt" that person so we can tell them what we think. This is especially true for people in positions of authority, such as sports officials. Listening shows respect, so train yourself to be a good listener.

- **Empathy is a powerful tool.** It is mentally putting you into another person's circumstances to experience it through their eyes. Make sure you don't just empathize, but also demonstrate your empathy through your words and non-verbal gestures. You can do this by using techniques such as making eye contact with the person and nodding your head in understanding. You can also use words such as "I understand what you are saying" and "I hear what you are saying."
- **Paraphrasing is repeating back what the person is saying to you in your own words.** This allows you to interrupt the person without them becoming angry or frustrated. This is because they will listen to what you are saying because it's what they are saying. Paraphrasing helps to convey empathy and it clarifies an understanding of what is causing the conflict.
- **When you have discussions with players and coaches and the time allows the discussion, you must summarize your decisions.** This creates decisiveness on your part. It also shows your competence and assertiveness in managing the game. By summarizing, you are making sure that they understand the call or decision you made. If you don't fill in the blanks of your decision, they will fill them in for you, which will create more confusion.

Chapter 6

Redirections (Handle The Outbursts Professionally)

Have you ever heard this said to an official during a game (in any sport)? "How can you make that call? You're terrible, you don't belong out here!" That's just one of many examples of something someone says derogatory or antagonistic to an official during a game. Many officials will ignore statements like this and continue to officiate. That's fine if it's a general statement coming from a fan. But what if it's a coach arguing a call during a dead ball or time out situation? Should you eject him? Maybe that would be appropriate. But if you decide an ejection isn't warranted and now you are engaged in a discussion with the coach, how do you respond to the outburst they just had and redirect their behavior so you can get them to comply, cooperate and/or collaborate? You handle it by maintaining your emotional equilibrium and having a pre-planned response to their outburst.

When a coach or player has an outburst, and it amounts to a verbal assault on you, you have a few response choices. One choice would be some sort of sanction for the person. Every official has his limits. These limits may be discretionary or they may be non-discretionary. Every sport also has its limits. In other words, some instances (like profanity) are going to result in an ejection or maybe a technical foul. There is no discretion in that decision. Other instances may leave you with some discretion, such as a coach telling you "that call was terrible" or "you should be better than that."

When you decide to respond to the person you also have some choices. The first choice is a natural reaction to the verbal assault. A natural reaction will lead to a confrontation. All you are doing is throwing gasoline on the fire. Here's an example of a natural response to the example above: "I made the call by blowing my whistle. So sit down and shut up." If you think that's not realistic, I beg to differ. I've heard this from officials. If what you want to say to the coach or player makes you feel good to say, then it's probably not the right thing to say. This thinking does not sit well with some officials.

Let me explain why it's in your best interest to forgo the natural reaction for a pre-planned professional response such as this: "I hear what you're saying coach but he didn't have position on the rebound. So let's get back to playing this game." That's an acknowledgment that you heard what they have said, followed by professional language. This is called a word block. You blocked the initial verbal assault and followed it up with professional language designed to achieve a specific goal. You showed assertiveness versus meekness (meekness can lead you to the possibility of becoming a bully magnet).

Let's take another example: You make a close or controversial call during a game and the coach gets excited and starts to voice his disapproval. You respond by saying, "What's your problem coach?" Or maybe you tell him to "settle down." We call these Anti-Peace Phrases. These types of phrases have the opposite effect of generating compliance, cooperation or collaboration. They add fuel to the resistance. Think about the last time you had an argument with your significant other, close friend or family member. How did telling them to "calm down" work for you? When coaches and players feel they are right and have been wronged, they feel disrespected when they hear these phrases. Try using phrases like: "Hold on coach, we can talk about the call," or "Time out coach, let's talk about this." These phrases are Peace Phrases. They are designed to treat the coaches and players with dignity by showing them respect. It allows you to begin your explanation of the call or decision you made. It doesn't matter whether their excitement over the call is justified, you still need to redirect that excitement so you can address the reason they became excited. Otherwise the conflict will escalate, maybe reaching a point of an ejection. We would like to try and avoid that.

We need to further examine the natural reaction versus a preplanned response. First, ask yourself this question when you put the uniform on for whatever sport you officiate: "Who do I represent?" In every class I teach for Vistelar, I ask this question. Here are some answers that I receive: yourself, other officials, your local/state official associations, all officials in that sport, the conference I officiate in.

Now, let's assume you find out that your response is on video when you tell the coach to "shut-up." It is estimated in the business world that seventeen persons are told about a negative employee contact that is seen by only one person. During an athletic event, how many people witnessed what you said? Pretend your video goes to You Tube and gets 10,000 hits. How did you look on that video? Do the math. How did you represent yourself? You need to consider how your family, people from your church or work saw you in this video. You have to be able to look at yourself in the mirror and say that what you did was right. No one cares what caused you to say what you said or that you got the call right. They only hear what you have said and see what you did. If you have taken the coaches behavior and minimized it with your bad response, the focus is on you instead of the game.

Another complicating factor associated with your natural reaction is that you caused the other person to posture in front of their team and fans. The definition of "posture" is to behave affectedly or unnaturally in order to impress others. If you begin arguing with a player or coach, you run the risk of escalating the situation. They have to come back with something that makes them look good because you just embarrassed them. You started out looking good with the right call and now you have "colored it bad" with your unprofessional response to the coach.

When people verbally assault you, they will attack your ego. They want to get to your Personal Face. People will attack your sex, race, age, size and skill level. Once they get to your Personal Face, you begin to lose your power. So what do you do to combat this? The answer is to identify your weakness. Your weakness is what sets you off. Once you identify it, name it. This will allow you to control your weakness. Here are some examples of what I have named. When I hear "that's not your call" from a coach, fan or player, I think to myself "there's Mr. Umpire Mechanics." If I hear "be consistent" I say to myself "it's the consistency police." These little phrases, which you say to yourself, will reduce your stress level and allow you to regain your focus.

Why should you choose to use a pre-planned professional response (redirection) versus that natural reaction that may sound good to you? Deflecting the outburst with professional language makes you feel good. You will also sound good to everyone listening or watching a video of the game. You don't want to argue with a player or coach. You also want to avoid arguing with fans. I once had a law enforcement colleague of mine say that "arguing with the public is like fighting a nuclear war, there are no winners." By using word blocks you re-direct the behavior so you can continue the game. Another benefit is that it dis-empowers the person who verbally assaults you. They are trying to find that "on ramp" to your ego. If they know that you heard them and that it didn't affect you (you deflected it) then they will probably stop.

One final thought on handling outbursts with a planned response. You have to practice it. I know there are officials that say "I do this" or "I know how to do this." The question you have to ask yourself is "can I do this under stress without messing up?" That's the key to success and assures that you won't say something inappropriate.

Chapter 6 Learning Points

- **There will be emotional outbursts at some level during a game.** Not all outbursts require an immediate response from an official. Some outbursts are "one and done." Other outbursts may require a response from you. These occur when there are repetitive comments coming from the bench or dugout, or when the coach comes out to argue a call. Remember that if you don't address the repetitive outburst, they will continue in intensity. By dealing with them early in the game, you will eliminate problems that could occur later in the game.
- **Using your "natural language" to respond to verbal assaults is never good.** We all would like to come back with a funny counter-punch to what is being said to us. That's not being professional. Arguing with the player or coach will cause them to posture and increase the intensity of the argument. Remember this: "If it makes you feel good to say it, it probably isn't the right thing to say." Use professional language to deflect the verbal assault and then re-direct the discussion so you can get the game going without any ejections (if possible).
- **Not everyone is prepared to handle a verbal assault.** You have to train yourself to respond professionally. Have a pre-planned practiced response in mind. Responses to verbal assaults need to be scripted. Then they need to be practiced. This assures that you can perform them under stress, when someone is right up in your face. That way you can assure a professional response on your part. Remember that you could be on video. You want to look good.

Chapter 7

Ethical Intervention: Bystander Mobilization

(Intervene To Prevent Bad Behavior)

Sports officials come in all shapes and sizes. They are business men and women, blue collar workers, public service workers, public safety professionals and teenagers (to name just a few). They come from all walks of life and are a cross-section of the human race. Therefore they are flawed. They are subject to all of the emotions that coaches, players and fans may exhibit during a game. Sometimes officials find themselves experiencing the same emotions that players, coaches and fans experience during the game. One of these emotions is anger, a strong feeling of annoyance, displeasure or hostility. They can lose control just like anyone else can. That's why it becomes so important for officials to watch out for each other in these types of situations.

So what happens when an official loses control and says or does something during the game that is inexcusable? It happens on all levels, in all sports. Ask yourself this question. Can a professional lose control? The answer is no. If professionals lose control, then they are no longer professionals. If you want to take that next step toward being a professional then you have to adopt the mind-set of being your fellow official's keeper, as they are ours. When you see bad things start to happen during the game, then you need to intervene. You can't stand there and let it happen and then later say "it wasn't me….it was my partner."

I'm not talking about making a wrong call or a bad decision. I'm talking about saying inappropriate things to people and doing things that are clearly inappropriate (such as making physical contact with players, coaches or fans). In order to intervene, you have to recognize that there is a problem and have a plan to intervene. This isn't easy to do because we all have egos and it's hard for someone to step in for us when our egos are damaged.

As we have discussed already, media has changed how conflict is depicted in society. It's no longer the bad behavior that is described in a newspaper article. It's now how many times bad behavior is viewed in the media. At no time in history has the behavior of people in positions of authority (sports officials) become more public. There are no places to hide your bad behavior when you officiate a game.

At Vistelar we like to say "there are no dark alleys to hide in anymore." It's probably going to be on video, which means that it's not going away. Some people may think that's not fair. It may not be, but that's the reality. If you don't want to be seen on video doing or saying "bad" things, then don't do or say "bad" things. Never before has the need for professional conduct been more important. We as officials need to act, talk and be more professional than ever before.

This is all about being ethical. I received a lot of training in ethics during my career as a law enforcement officer. We took an ethical oath and I taught ethics as a law enforcement instructor. The best explanation of ethics comes from Jack Hoban, a retired United States Marine who taught and trained martial arts and ethics to the Marine Corps. Jack continues to train through his training group Resolution Group International (RGI). As Jack teaches, ethics are actions and morals are feelings (right and wrong). It's moral for someone to feel that bullying another person is wrong. It's ethical to take action to stop the bullying. He also states that "ethics are moral values in action." If you see something inappropriate that your partner did and you report it (either verbally or a written report), then you are ethical. If you took it one step further and you stepped in and stopped it, then you are an ethical protector. You protected your partner and maybe a player, coach or fan. The challenge for officials is deciding when you have to intervene.

The concept of Bystander Mobilization was created by Jill Weisensel. Jill is a Training Consultant for Vistelar and a lieutenant for the Department of Public Safety at Marquette University. As Jill explains, the decision by a bystander to intervene hinges on two important factors. The first is whether the bystander feels she has a responsibility to act. My answer to that for officials is yes, you have that responsibility. The second factor is whether or not the bystander feels she is capable of acting. You can overcome this doubt (if you have the doubt) by adopting that mind-set of being your fellow official's keeper. Then you have to train yourself and have a plan on how to intervene.

Before we get into the actual tactics on how to intervene in bad situations, let's examine the responsibility to intervene that you have as an official. If you are working with a partner, or in a crew of officials, no one is innocent if they watch something inappropriate happen and don't intervene when they have the ability to do so. Our duty during the game is to assist our fellow officials in managing the game. What happens when something goes wrong and we can fix it? When appropriate, we get together to discuss the call or ruling and make changes as warranted. But what if we see our partner begin to "melt down?" It's our duty to either prevent the meltdown from happening or to prevent it from getting any worse. Finally, if it rises to the level of needing to file a report with an appropriate person, then file the report.

Once you have adopted the mindset that you will be an "ethical protector," you then must have a plan for how to accomplish this. These three strategies for Ethical Intervention can help you to formulate such a plan:

1. Professional Intervention: Pre-Incident Prevention
2. Direct Intervention: Contact Official Override
3. Delayed: Post-Incident Remedies

Regardless of what level or age group you are officiating, you want to do a good job. If you choose to officiate your sport at a higher level, you have to develop professionally. To be professional, you have to be ethical. The first step in being ethical happens way before you begin to officiate that game. Pre-incident prevention begins with raising and maintaining your ethical presence. Make that decision to learn as much as you can about officiating. Make that decision that you want to look good, sound good and be good when you officiate a game.

Let's go back to the Showtime tactic. Showtime allows you to put on your Professional Face and it gets you into the mindset of using professional language. It prepares you to "present your ethical presence on the field." You develop a reputation that says you are fair and impartial and that you maintain your emotional equilibrium. Once you have mastered maintaining your own personal ethical presence, you begin to have an effect on other people. You all positively impact your partners, the players and the coaches. It's contagious.

The second strategy is Direct Ethical Interventions. It is referred to as Contact Official Override. The official that is engaged in verbalization with the player, coach or fan is considered the Contact Official. The other official(s) is considered the Cover Official. The job of the Cover Official is to do just that. Cover the back for the Contact Official. This means that you keep everyone else at that game from entering into the discussion that your partner is having with the player and coach. The communication should be one-to-one with no external noise coming from other players or coaches. We refer to this concept as "one voice".

Let's say something begins to happen and you need to intervene. The first level is to verbally intervene. The Cover Official simply talks to his partner, the Contact Official. You can develop verbal cues, such as saying "Showtime." Or you can say "Be careful partner." This brings your partner back to reality and gives him a clue that he is or is about to do or say something bad. You can develop your own cues for your partner, especially if you work with certain people all of the time. Another tactic is to simply say "Knock it off." The credit for "Knock it off" goes to Harry Dolan, retired Chief of Police of the Raleigh, North Carolina Police Department. Chief Dolan says that when someone's actions or comments are inconsistent with your mission, than tell them to "knock it off."

Taking over the conversation is another tactic in Direct Intervention. We call this "tapping out." You accomplish this by simply tapping your partner on the shoulder and saying "I've got this." You want to separate them from the person who is getting to their Personal Face.

The second level of intervention occurs when your partner is not responding to the verbal intervention cues. You now have to position yourself in a way that separates your partner from whomever they are arguing with. This is a tactic that is probably most recognized by fans because you can see it. One official has either ejected someone or sanctioned them in some way. The player or coach says something to the official and they become engaged in a face-to-face argument. The Cover Official(s) moves in and separates the Contact Official and player or coach. I have discussed this with my partners. We refer to this as "peeling off." Everyone has their own tactics and terms for their use in their particular sport. It's all a matter of opinion on what tactic to use. Pick the one that separates the antagonist and prevents the incident from escalating. Don't stand there and watch your partner melt down.

The third level of intervention occurs when things have gone really bad and you sense that there is going to be physical contact (bumping, pushing or shoving). Violence in sports has become more prevalent in recent years. Although it doesn't happen often, it can be disastrous when it does. Therefore we have to be sure it's safe to intervene physically. The intervention tactic that is used has to be well thought out and practiced. If you don't do this right, you could be the one that gets elbowed in the face, or in an extreme circumstance, punched in the face (or worse). This hurts, even if it was deemed to be a reaction to you grabbing them. People who are angry can fall off of the tracks of common sense and decency and become violent. They can throw an elbow or a punch without conscious thought. You don't want to be on the receiving end of that elbow or punch.

I was the home plate umpire of a college baseball game in which both teams left their benches and began a brawl on the field. I'll never forget that feeling of helplessness as I stood against the fence watching this take place. In the end, a statistician from one of the teams was punched in the face by the pitching coach from the other team. His nose was broken by the punch. I never was able to talk to that coach, but one of my good friends and umpire partners did talk to him. According to him, the coach stated he was trying to pull some players apart when he felt someone "on his back." He instinctively turned and punched whoever it was that was on his back. This was a real mess. It just goes to show you what can happen when bad things start happening to people who have no plan.

The third strategy of Ethical Intervention occurs when the situation is over. What was said or done is over. You can't change it, but you can try and repair or minimize the damage that may have occurred. This is called a Delayed Intervention. These are post-incident remedies. The first thing to do is to apologize when it is appropriate. You are not apologizing for missing a call or messing up a rule interpretation. You are apologizing for something you may have said or done that was wrong. You are simply showing class.

The next remedy would be to debrief the incident with your partner(s). Do this even if you didn't find it necessary to apologize. Debriefing will be discussed in more detail later. There can be some hard feelings when someone over-rides your behavior. Remember that we all have egos. You can repair the egos and maintain your professionalism when you bring what happened out in the open and discuss it. I would rather have my partner yell at me after the game than yell at a player or coach. If they don't get it later (you were protecting them), then you probably don't want them as a partner.

The last remedy is to self-report the incident to a supervisor. This supervisor may be a conference commissioner, athletic director, state association or an assigner. It is much better for you if they hear from you and not from someone else.

Chapter 7 Learning Points

- **Sports Officials came in all shapes and sizes.** We are all human. Therefore we are flawed and subject to the same behaviors and emotions that coaches and players may exhibit. One of these emotions is anger. We can't let that happen, but it does. Our partners can prevent us from melting down and doing something unprofessional. Develop the mindset that you are your fellow official's keeper, as they are ours. Let's watch each other's backs.

- **Be an Ethical Protector.** Recognize something is wrong and intervene if it is safe to do so. Don't just stand there and watch your partner do something unprofessional. If you allow it to happen in your presence and you could have prevented it, you are just as guilty. You have a duty to intervene when you see bad things start to happen between players, coaches and officials. Don't run and hide!
- **There are three levels to intervention.** The first is Pre-Incident Prevention. Raise your own ethical presence by acting professionally, all of the time. The second intervention is Direct Intervention-Contact Official Override. Be alert and observe when your partner is in crisis. Then step in and prevent it from getting worse. Be careful when stepping into situations of physical violence. You may get hurt if you don't have a pre-planned practiced response. The third intervention is delayed-Post Incident Remedies. The situation is over and the damage was done. You can minimize the damage by showing some "class" and apologizing when appropriate. You must also debrief the incident with your partner(s) and report it to your supervisor.

Chapter 8

Persuasion (Keeping The Players And Coaches In The Game)

Before I talk about the Persuasion Sequence, I want to quickly review the Five Maxims of Communications:

1. Listen With All Your Senses;
2. Ask, Don't Tell Someone To Do Something;
3. Explain Why They Are Being Asked-Set Context;
4. Offer Options, Not Threats;
5. Give A Second Chance.

I am going to tie these in with the Persuasion Sequence so you can see how it all fits.

The Persuasion Sequence is a tactic designed to gain compliance, cooperation and/or collaboration when you meet verbal resistance. This tactic is commonly used in two situations relative to officiating.

The first is when you ask someone to do something. One example of this would be asking a coach to keep his players on the sideline under control. The other situation would occur when you explain a ruling or call that you made. In either situation, you attempt to gain that compliance, cooperation and/or collaboration through the use of the Persuasion Sequence. Here it is:

1. Ask
2. Set Context
3. Give Options
4. Confirm Non-compliance
5. Take Appropriate Action

Before we go through the sequence, let's examine the reason why this tactic is necessary. We have already discussed the emotions involved in athletics and that coaches and players may posture in front of their peers and the fans. They become "difficult people." A difficult person will always tell you no when asked to do something, or he will continue to question your ruling or call. It's going to take some persuasion on your part and an explanation that is done the right way before he is going to comply, cooperate and/or collaborate. The Persuasion Sequence provides the tactics to help you to persuade them. Nine out of ten people will work with you if you perform the Persuasion Sequence the right way. The nicest people will posture and want explanations. Remember question one of the "Four Great American Questions?" They want to know "why." As a law enforcement officer, I found it rare that someone would immediately accept my request to do something without some sort of explanation. As an umpire, I have experienced the same reaction from players and coaches.

The first step in the Persuasion Sequence is to "ask." You are simply asking someone to do something using an interrogatory tone of voice. "Coach, can you have your players please stay behind the line?" This is an ethical appeal that is backed up by a rule or accepted guidelines and behaviors. Don't make up rules or start asking them to do things that don't make any sense. Remember that people want to be asked rather than told what to do (Maxim #2).

After asking, let's assume you don't get a response or you have to start explaining the rule or decision that you have made. You are going to have to move to the second step which is to "set context." By setting the context you are explaining why you are asking them to do something or why you made that ruling or decision (Maxim #3). "Coach, I made that call because he failed to step off the rubber before he separated his hands. That's a balk." Use a declaratory tone of voice. This is a rational appeal based on facts and rules. The rational appeal is logical. But remember that people don't think logically when they are angry and upset.

There are three components to setting context. The first is to explain the actual ruling or call that you made. The second is to explain why you made the call or why the rule exists (if appropriate). "Coach, he separated his hands before he stepped off the rubber. That deceives the batter and the runner." The third component is to ask them if they understand the rule (if appropriate). State only what you need to state and don't include feelings and emotions.

This is an area where you can get yourself into trouble if you make things up and start to talk too much. There are people who will try to trick you into a response that doesn't match your decision or call. This is a "sneaky" person. They present a nice, cooperative persona and then become difficult when things aren't going their way. Just explain your decision or why you asked something of them, and wait for their response.

There are officials who would say that explanations are not needed. I would clarify this statement to say that they are not "always" needed. You don't have to explain every call. But when players and coaches ask questions about calls, or they dispute the calls, you show them respect by giving an explanation. How detailed your explanation gets (the second and third parts of setting context) is dependent on the situation itself.

This came up when I was training new umpires for our association. I had a gentleman who was probably in his late 50's. He umpired when he was younger. He stopped umpiring for several years and decided he wanted to get back into it. We were running a drill for base umpires that involved making calls at first base. The drill involved making safe calls at first base when the first baseman pulls his foot off the bag too early on a force play. The mechanic involved was to make an appropriate safe call and then indicate that he was off the base when he caught the ball.

The gentleman came over to me and said, "I was told when I attended umpire training years ago that we didn't have to explain our calls. Why do we have to indicate he was off of the base?' I asked him if he ever made a call like that. He stated yes. I then asked him if the coach came out to question it. He stated yes. I then explained that was why we make the indication he was off of the base. It answers the coach's question before he can even ask it. Hence he stays in the dugout (unless he felt he wasn't off the base).

The third step in the Persuasion Sequence is to "give options." You may not even have to use this step if the coach or player accepts your explanation on the ruling or call, or does what you ask them. But for the sake of explanation in this sequence, let's assume you haven't made any progress. You give options using a service-oriented tone of voice (Maxim #4). This is your personal appeal that relates directly to the person you are talking to. It utilizes the "Greed Principal," which states that "if the person has something to win or lose, than you have something to use."

So you start with a positive option first. Give them something that amounts to a win for them. "Coach, I'm not going to change the call. This is a good game. Let's keep you in the game and get going (Question #4 - What's in it for me?). If that doesn't work, you have to move to the negative option. "Coach, if you don't leave the field, I'm going to have to eject you." Always give the positive option first. If you start with a negative option, they will focus on the negative option and never hear the positive option. If neither option works, then go back to the positive option with a twist. "Coach, let's get the game going and keep you in the game. I don't want have to eject you. Will you work with me here?" If it's not working, let's go to step four.

The fourth step in the Persuasion Sequence is to "confirm non-compliance." Nothing has worked and you have to get the game going. You confirm non-compliance through the use of a collaborative tone of voice. This is a practical appeal. You are making one last appeal through the use of an offbeat strategy. "Coach is there anything I can say to get you to go back to the bench? Work with me here." In this step you are giving them that second chance we discussed in Maxim #5. The decision is up to them. If they are ejected, it's because they chose to be ejected.

The final step is to "Take Appropriate Action." This is the time you would call a technical foul, eject, present a red card, throw a flag or do whatever is appropriate in your sport. At this point, officials should refer to the rules and standards that are applicable in the sport for a given situation. In the scenario I went through, the coach chose to be ejected. The coach or player was given every opportunity to curb his behavior. If you chose to sanction them, then it was their decision. Realize that at any time during the Persuasion Sequence the player or coach can accept your ruling and move on. They can also escalate their behavior that may cause you to sanction them at that point in the sequence. These are fluid situations.

Chapter 8 Learning Points

- **We encounter "Difficult People" every day in our lives.** Athletics is not an exception. When you handle it properly (the Persuasion Sequence), a "Difficult Person" will comply with what you are asking them to do. It may take steps 2, 3 and 4 of persuasion sequence until they get the right picture. This typically happens 90% of the time. The important thing to remember is to "do it the right way".

- **Setting the context for your decisions shows respect.** You do not have to explain every call or decision you make during the game. But when it's time to do it, you have to know the rules and be able to articulate why you made a call. There are coaches and players who will bait you into answers. That's why having a pre-planned response to situations is critical. Stick to the facts.
- **Everyone wants an option when they are being asked to do something.** There are good options and there are bad options. When you offer options you are essentially opening a box that the coach and players have trapped themselves in. They can feel that they have a choice in the situation. Make sure you start with the good options. Using the negative options first is viewed as threats. They will only focus on the negative option, react to it and never hear the good option. This answers that fourth question, "what's in it for me?"
- **Before you take action, such as an ejection, confirm that they are not going to return to the bench or stop the behavior.** This is your chance to make a practical appeal. No official should like ejecting coaches and players from a game. That's when it becomes personal and not professional. Yet there are times when it needs to happen. Giving them that second chance is essentially their last chance -- shows respect. It also makes you look good.
- **Following the Persuasion Sequence keeps the discussion from going around in circles.** It fixes a limit on the amount of time that you are going to spend discussing a call. You can

do everything right when you are talking to them and they still won't be convinced. Remember, being right doesn't always convince a person who feels they have been wronged.

Chapter 9

When Words Alone Fail

(When Is It Time To Act-Eject or Sanction)

Unfortunately not every conflict in athletics can be resolved through the use of verbal skills. There are instances when using verbal skills is clearly not effective or appropriate. We call this "When Words Alone Fail." Let's first review the "classroom model" description of "When Words Alone Fail":

- If the Persuasion Sequence has not worked or would be clearly inappropriate;
- If there are safety issues based on a danger to yourself or others, danger to property under your control, flight or revised priorities.

When I speak to athletic groups or teach this course to officials, I am always asked the question that sounds something like this: "Do you expect me to talk to someone that just said or did whatever?"

My answer is "no."

We don't expect you talk to someone who is punching another player. Nor do we expect you to persuade a coach who just told you "You are an incompetent (you can fill in the blanks here)." These are situations that leave the official with little or no discretion to act. But there are also situations that are not as clear-cut. They involve some discretion by an official. It's hard to describe what level of discretion is needed and what the limits are. It can vary from sport to sport, level of competition and from official to official. In any case, let's take a crack at it and try and set some limits. To start off, let's break down the classroom model listed above and apply it to situations in athletics.

Let's first talk about the SAFETY issues. First and foremost, we don't want violence occurring during our games. Here are some examples of safety issues:

- Coach or player intentionally makes physical contact with you;
- Players or coaches assaulting officials;
- Players fighting or extremely dangerous play;
- Coaches fighting with players or other coaches;
- Players, coaches and fans fighting

You get the idea. We don't expect you to talk when these kinds of things are taking place.

There are times when players and coaches turn their frustration and anger toward inanimate objects. This includes throwing chairs, kicking balls, breaking tables, throwing bases and breaking equipment to list just a few. As an official, think of yourself as safeguarding this property that is essentially under your control during that game. That refers to the previous bullet point that states "danger to property under your control."

There will also be instances when the coach or player walks away from you (flight) during your conversation. They either accepted your explanation or they just gave up. It would be pointless to keep talking because they are no longer there to listen to what you are saying. Let them go and continue the game.

You may also have other priorities that would preclude having long discussions about your calls or rulings during the game. These priorities are usually related to weather and issues of darkness. If it's raining and the conditions of the field are deteriorating, you probably don't want to spend a lot of time talking. Therefore you have "revised priorities." I've had this happen several times while umpiring. I let the coach know that we are under weather or time constraints and we need to get the game going. Remember to show them respect by explaining to them why you can't spend a lot of time talking about a call or ruling.

The last situation in which you no longer need to talk is when the Persuasion Sequence clearly is not working. The coach or player is not going along with your call or ruling, and you need to act. You have asked them, explained to them why you made the call or ruling, you have given them options, you have confirmed that they are not going to comply (the second chance!) and now you have to take action. You are not required to keep repeating yourself. You tried, it didn't work.

The choice on what happens next is up to the player or coach. You have treated them respectfully and you have given them a chance to continue without being ejected or sanctioned. You looked good, you sounded good and you acted professionally.

These concepts can be the hardest things for new sports officials to master. It's just not natural to be able to eject someone from a game. When you add in other factors such as gender (female officials) and age (young officials) it becomes even harder for a new official. The young official may have to sanction an adult coach. The female official may have to sanction a male coach. These are both challenging situations for the officials. If you become passive and fail to respond appropriately you could essentially become a "bully magnet" which could lead to your loss of control during the game. You can also be overly aggressive by responding too quickly and harshly. You over-emphasize your authority and begin losing credibility and respect.

I never found it easy to eject someone from a baseball game. No official should like doing this, but sometimes it is necessary. And when you do it, you are going to have to explain what you did. Use the model of "When Words Alone Fail" to justify your actions to your supervisors and peers. It will also assist you in your report writing and your review of the incident.

Chapter 9 Learning Points

- **Not every conflict situation can or should be handled with words.** Some instances require actions, such as ejections. Experienced officials understand this and establish their own guidelines to help them make these decisions. Newer officials need guidelines when they first start officiating. When Words Alone Fail helps you to define the time when you need to act instead of talk.

- **Safety is paramount.** You and your partner's safety, along with the players and coaches, should leave you no discretion in deciding when to act. We do not expect you to talk to someone who is jeopardizing someone's safety.
- **In the situations outlined in this chapter, officials can run the risk of either over-reacting to a situation or under-reacting to a situation.** Use the guidelines discussed to guide you in your decisions of when to act. This will also help you explain why you may have ejected someone during the game.

Chapter 10

Review and Reporting (Improve Everyone's Performance)

The final component of the Verbal Defense & Influence program is to review and report what occurred during the game. The review is simply asking ourselves how we did. Every official should review his or her performance personally and with their partners or supervisors. Let's refer to this as debriefing.

Debriefing is an integral part of improving your performance as an official. When done appropriately, it can enhance an official's performance. When done inappropriately, it creates a defensive atmosphere and is counter-productive to enhancing performance. Debriefing also allows you to create an outline for any incident that may have to be reported either verbally or in written form.

There are all types of performance debriefings that take place in each of the sports we officiate. They can range from a formal debriefing that consists of rating systems that allow an official to move from a lower level of officiating to a higher level of officiating. Or they can be an informal debriefing that takes place between members of their crew and/or supervisors. The debriefing may involve your general performance during the game or it may involve a particular situation that occurred during the game. Either way there should be a process followed that is designed to improve performance while not tearing down an official.

The first step in debriefing should be a "wellness" check to make sure that everyone is okay. Some officials may view this as being silly. I would beg to differ. The emotional well being of an official is important for future performance. I believe it is why many new officials don't come back for a second year. They simply get "fed up" with being yelled at.

Different things happen in every sport. Conflicts can occur during a game and these conflicts have an effect on an official. It's how well you handle the conflict that will determine how you can learn from the conflict so you flourish as an official. It is important that we review our experiences and our performance and discuss it. The best example of this comes at the earliest level of umpires that I train.

The Wisconsin Umpires Association (WUA) offers a course for first and second year umpires. The training director for the WUA, John Promersberger, is an accomplished high school and college umpire in both softball and baseball. He and I have had many discussions on the importance of getting our umpires to return for a second year, especially the younger umpires. This is the main reason the WUA has incorporated the VDI training into their program. Every year, I ask the second year umpires what their biggest issue was and they respond by saying "dealing with the coaches and fans." John watches a lot of youth games during a season and he speaks to the umpires. He hears the same concerns from the umpires he speaks to. They are discouraged by the behavior of the parents and coaches. They felt helpless so we focused on providing them with the strategies to deal with the issues that caused them the most stress.

After we check on everyone's wellness, we ask the question, "How do you think you did?" The majority of people will tell you what they did wrong or what they could improve on. Once they finish their assessment of themselves, you can give your assessment of how they did.

Begin with the positive (just like the Persuasion Sequence). Tell them what they did right. If you lead off with the negative they will most likely internalize that and not hear anything else that you have to say. Also stay away from using that self-referential language that uses the word "I." Don't "big league" them by telling them how great you are and what you would have done in that situation.

Remember, it's not all about you. It's about them and how they can improve. Have the person tell you what he needs to do to improve his performance. If you are officiating with more than two people, this is the point where others can add their input. Finally, sum up what you just went over and leave everyone feeling better than they were. This sets up the best scenario to improve future performance.

The idea of debriefing also relates to coaches and players. You want to leave them feeling better than they were feeling at their worst, whenever possible. I get it, that's hard for them when they have lost. But consider this. You may see them again. People will remember how they were treated the last time they had an interaction with you. We refer to this as the Closure Principle. If they feel they have been disrespected, then there's a good chance the next game will be filled with tension.

The process of debriefing a player or coach isn't as clear-cut as debriefing your partner. You aren't going to stand next to a coach and ask him how he thinks he did. The process for players and coaches takes place during the entire encounter. When you utilize the tactics discussed in this book you will treat them with dignity by showing them respect. This will result in a better encounter the next time you see them. Here are some points to consider in understanding the Closure Principle:

- Always utilize and keep your Professional Face. This allows you to keep emotional equilibrium, which helps you to convey respect;
- Remember to exercise the Platinum Rule - Treat others the way you would like to be treated...under similar circumstances;
- Never inflate people with adrenaline. Don't throw gasoline on a fire. If you display anger it will be given back to you "tenfold";
- Being flexible and showing strength is used to generate voluntary compliance, cooperation or collaboration (3 C's). Being rigid and showing it is a weakness that generates resistance;
- Redirect the emotional outbursts with the use of professional language to accomplish professional goals. When you show resistance to the outburst you will have a difficult time gaining the 3 C's.

These are all things that have been researched and proven to work in the real world. They will assist you in achieving the proper closure with the coaches and players so your next encounter can be a positive encounter.

As an official, there will be times when you must report an incident that occurred during a game. It may be an ejection, player behavior, coach behavior or fan behavior. It is important that you report incidents such as ejections and bad behavior so that people are held accountable for their actions.

When officials get into group settings with their peers, all sorts of stories are told about bad behavior that occurred during the game. When I hear these stories, and they appear to be situations that need to be reported, I ask the person, "Did you report it?" Too many times the answer is "no." That's a bad answer. Now, the report may be verbal, but often times it is a written report that is required by the organization you represent. So how do you begin to write a report?

First, debriefing the incident with your partner and/or crew helps you form the outline for your report. The report needs to be an account of what occurred before the incident, what occurred during the incident and what occurred after the incident. When someone evaluates how you handled an incident, they will not be looking at it as a photograph -- coach said this, so I did that.

It is now looked at as a full-length feature film with the beginning, middle and end. The beginning describes what caused the conflict (a call, a ruling). You may list the behaviors you observed and the things that were said by the coach and player. You then would list the tactics you used to achieve one of the 3C's. Be specific in stating what you said. This is the point where the Persuasion Sequence serves as an outline. You asked something, you set the context by explaining the call, you gave positive options, then negative options, you confirmed non-compliance (they continued the behavior) and then you acted (maybe an ejection). Then list what happened after you ejected (sanctioned the person).

The people reading the report want to know why you ejected someone, why you restricted someone to a bench or why you forfeited a game or red carded someone. You are justifying your actions. The report should present the reader with the facts that support why you couldn't talk to them anymore or that talking was clearly inappropriate or it just didn't work.

Chapter 10 Learning Points

- **Debrief your and your team's performance after a game.** Your review should include your performance relative to mechanics and positioning. It should also include the calls and rulings that were made. Finally, review how any conflicts were handled. This will reinforce how you've trained and expose any deficiencies that you and your crew may need to improve on.
- **The sequence used in debriefing is important.** First, make sure everyone is "ok" after the game. Then have each team member evaluate themselves. Start with positives and then the negatives. Avoid making the debriefing a personal attack on someone's ability to officiate.
- **Remember the Closure Principal.** Leave people feeling better than they were at their worst. This is hard when teams have

lost a game. But, if you treat them with respect during the game they will remember it the next time you officiate their games. This increases your chances of have a good game the next time you meet.

- **Debriefing helps you to create an outline for any reports that you may have to write after the game.** You are simply getting your facts right. Don't just focus on the ejection. Describe what led to the conflict, what occurred during the conflict and how you responded to the conflict. It's not a photograph of what happened; it's a full-length movie.

Chapter 11

Conclusion (How Do We Improve Our Performance?)

So where do we go from here? I hope your reading of this book has made you aware of the benefits the Verbal Defense & Influence program can have for sports officials. Reading this book amounts to a "fire talk." You now have to conduct the "fire drills." You have to practice the skills. It takes three to five thousand repetitions to become proficient in that skill. You can read about this in the Appendix section of this book-what Vistelar calls Emotionally Safe Performance Driven Instruction.

Vistelar offers a wide range of programs, from speaking engagements, to 4- to 8-hour workshops to 20-hour practitioner courses. The longer the program is, the more time that's devoted to practicing the skills. If you would like to become a VDI instructor, you can attend the 32-hour Instructor Development Course.

As the book outlined, the Communicating Under Pressure (CUP) card has ten components. In training different organizations and professions, I noticed one common theme with each class. There is usually one of the ten components that will benefit each individual the most. No one area is more important than another. But there may be one tactic (or more) that raised your eyebrows when you were reading this book. Take that tactic and start utilizing it. Think of the program as a mosaic. Mosaics are different colored glass tiles put together to form an image. The VDI program can be viewed as ten pieces put together to form a complete conflict management program.

At the end of every class or presentation, our trainers do two things. First, we ask the participants these questions: "What did you learn?" and "What's your plan?"

It's important to get these answers, because our commitment to you is that you walk away from your training sessions having learned a skill(s) that you can immediately utilize. Otherwise, we wasted your time. That's my challenge to you: Internalize the Five Maxim's of Communications. Then pick a tactic(s) and begin to practice the skill and put it work. You also have the option of contacting us at Vistelar to request more information on our programs. If you wish, you can contact me personally.

The second thing we do as instructors is review the feedback we receive relative to our presentations. This helps us improve the training, determine its relevance to your sport/situation and see how effective we have been in training you on these skills. We read and discuss all of the written evaluations. We then review our programs based on these evaluations. Our students teach us what is important. I also encourage you to review this book. Your honest reviews will make us better at what we do.

One last thing I needed to mention. You may have noticed how applicable the VDI tactics are to everyday life. These tactics transcend the professions we all work in. They apply to both our personal and professional lives. Use the tactics you have learned all the time. Use them at work, use them at home, and use them at the grocery store. Vistelar has powerful Peace Stories that we have recorded that prove the success of these tactics in all walks of life.

Gary Klugiewicz is one of the top Defensive Tactics Instructors in the country. Gary is also Vistelar's director of Training for Verbal Defense & Influence. In 2013, I assisted Gary in teaching a class at a large police department. This department was experiencing a lot of pain relative to its relationship with the community. The students were all dedicated professional members of the department who wanted to effect positive change. As Gary and I were reviewing the written evaluations we came across one that stated: "You saved my marriage". When we hear this type of feedback, we know we're heading down the right path, and that what we do isn't just about sports officiating. It's about applying the training and lessons to all walks of life to reduce conflict. We all gain from that. We will keep refining our lessons, and we hope to keep learning from you.

Appendix I

Tips On How To Practice The Skills

"There's a reason we conduct fire drills instead of fire talks"
- Gary Klugiewicz

Conducting drills will improve your ability to effectively communicate while under stress. The drills need to be done correctly. First you develop a script that contains professional language designed to meet the desired goal of generating voluntary compliance, co-operation and/or collaboration. Here's an example of a Universal Greeting that would occur during a pre-game meeting in baseball (ground rules):

- Appropriate Greeting - "*Hi coach.*"
- Introduce yourself - "*I'm your name.*"
- Explain the reason for the contact - "*Let's go over the ground rules.*"

- Ask a relevant question - "*First, can I see your line-up cards?*"

Here's an example of a Redirection script for football:

Coach Comment:

"That's a terrible call! He was not holding! You just cost us a first down! That call was absolute bull%$&#!

Official Response:

"Coach, I got it. You're not happy with that call but 64 had his hands outside of the shoulders. That's holding. Now please get back on the sidelines so we can get the game going."

These scripts should be realistic and relevant to the sport you officiate. You are beginning to practice "when/then" thinking that addresses the situations that will occur during the game.

Once you have created the script, follow these steps of the Verbal Defense & Influence Drill Format:

1. Have the students read the script to themselves.

2. The instructor and the students read the script out loud.

3. The students, in pairs, read the script to each other.

The first three steps in the Drill Format progressively prepare the student for success during the drills. This will improve their proficiency and instill confidence in their ability to communicate under stress.

The fourth step in the Drill Format is to conduct Triad Training. This would include one student acting as the official, one student acting as the player or coach and one student acting as an instructor/coach. There are four steps the instructor must complete in the Triad Training when they perform the drill;

1. Visually show the students what you want them to do.
2. Explain the drill to them.
3. Demonstrate the entire drill to the student.
4. Have the students teach the drill back to you.

Once these four steps are completed you can now conduct the drills. By following these steps you will eliminate any confusion on what is expected to be performed during the drills.

The final step in the Drill Format is to debrief the drills. Debriefing is broken down as follows;

1. The instructor/coach asks everyone if they are you okay. This is a wellness check designed to maintain an emotionally safe training environment.
2. The instructor/coach asks, "How do you think you did?" and "What happened?" The students often fix their own mistakes. According to Dave Young this is a sign that they are learning the skill. If they can't make the corrections, they have not learned the skill.
3. The instructor/coach gives a positive comment, if possible. Bring out the positive performance before addressing the mistakes.

4. The instructor/coach asks "What would you do different next time?" This is their chance to explain how they would correct any errors.

5. The instructor/coach, role player and/or peers can make comments that bring out the positives and the negatives.

6. The instructor/coach gives summation of the drill that includes all of the feedback received during the debriefing.

Once the debriefing is concluded the students switch roles and conduct another drill.

It is important not to skip steps and to follow the steps in order. According to Dave Young and Gary Klugiewicz the common mistake is to teach and combine too many skills, too fast. You will confuse and frustrate the students. Once this happens they begin to shut down and the learning stops.

If you would like to learn more about "Emotionally Safe Performance Driven Instruction," you can check out the Vistelar website at www.vistelar.com.

Appendix 2

Examples of Drills or Activities

Be Alert and Decisive/Respond, Don't React (Be Ready and Stay Safe)

10-5-2 Rule - Divide your officials into pairs. Measure out the distances so they can visualize what the distances are. Have them stand 10 feet, 5 feet and 2 feet from each other. Emphasize their hand positioning as the distances decrease to 2 feet. The hands should be at waist level or slightly above, with their palms open.

Each sport requires officials to sanction players and coaches in different ways. You can now add this tactic into the drill. The Triad Training Drill can now be utilized. For example in soccer you can now add the presentation of a red and or yellow card. For basketball it would be the technical foul mechanic and for football it would be the presentation of the flag.

Stop Sign - Divide your officials into pairs. Have them stand 10 feet from each other. One official plays the role of a player or coach. Have the player/coach move quickly toward the official while verbalizing their displeasure over a call. The official should place their hands at chest level with open palms and verbalize "Stop. What's the issue?" The player/coach then stops and the drill is concluded.

Emphasize to the officials that there should be no physical contact occurring during this drill. Keep the drill safe.

Thinker's Stance - Divide your officials into pairs. Have them stand 2 feet from each other. One official plays the role of the player/coach. Have the player coach dispute a call with the official. The official listens to what the player/coach is saying while in the "Thinker's Stance." The official should have their hand resting on their chin with the other hand supporting the elbow.

Five Maxims of Communications

Divide your officials into pairs. Give them the script below. Utilizing this script, the officials will explain the Five Maxims of Communications to each other.

Instead of focusing on how people are different, we should focus on how people are the same.

Unconditionally we will treat players and coaches with dignity by showing them respect, regardless of their behavior. Then, we will communicate with players and coaches based on a committment to these five maxims:

All players and coaches want to be:

1. Listened to with all of your senses.
2. Asked rather than being told to do something.
3. Told why they are being asked to do something.

4. Offered options rather than threats.

5. Given a second chance.

Treating players and coaches with dignity by showing them respect and listening with all your senses are unconditional - they apply to all situations.

Maxims 2 – 5 are conditional based on acceptable behavior and safety considerations.

Having said this, whenever possible:

We will ask players and coaches to do something rather than ordering them.

We will tell players and coaches why they are being asked to do something.

We will offer players and coaches options rather than threats.

We will give players and coaches a second chance to do something before taking appropriate action.

These Maxims are reflected in the Persuasion Sequence that states that, in order to attempt to generate voluntary compliance, cooperation, and/or collaboration a professional should:

1. Ask (them to do something), then, if necessary

2. Set Context (tell them why we want them to do something), then, if necessary

3. Offer Options (positive, then negative options), then, if necessary

4. Confirm Noncompliance, then, if necessary
5. Take Appropriate Action

Showtime

The Showtime drill should be performed while standing.

1. Stack up your blocks;
   - Ground your feet 4-6 in. apart. Drive them into the ground.
   - Relax your knees (bend slightly).
   - Tuck in your buttocks and drive your naval through your thoracic vertebrae (back).
   - Take in a deep breath to raise your rib cage off of your pelvis and to drive your scapula down.
2. Say "Showtime" to yourself
3. Breathe in, pause, breathe out, pause and repeat (each is usually a four second count)
4. Put on your Professional Face
5. Use the appropriate positive self-talk
6. Step into the arena and handle it

Universal Greeting

Every sport has a pre-game meeting with the officials, coaches and/or players. Therefore each sport can create a script for how these meetings are conducted. The script should include these steps, in order:

1. Appropriate Greeting- "Hi coach."

2. Introduce yourself- "I'm your name."

3. Explain the reason for the contact- "Let's check the equipment." Or "Let's go over the ground rules."

4. Ask a relevant question- "Can I see your line-up cards?"

Set-up this drill the same way the official would conduct a meeting in their respective sport. For example in baseball it would be two umpires and two coaches. For football it would be the referee and the captains conducting a coin toss. Have each official utilize the script and take the role of the official who conducts the pre-game meeting.

Beyond Active Listening

Beyond Active Listening is a tactic to develop a shared understanding of what the player or coach is thinking so that you can move from disagreement to compliance, cooperation or even collaboration.

This drill can be conducted by utilizing a video of a disagreement between a player or coach and an official. I have found many videos on social media that depict conflicts between coaches, players and officials. Find a video relative to the sport you officiate (if possible).

Divide the officials into groups of four or five (depending on class size). One person in the group is picked to record on paper what the group says. Show the video to the class and have them discuss it. Give them specific items to discuss relative to Beyond Active Listening.

1. Listening - Why was the coach or player disputing the call? Did the official interrupt the coach or player? Was the interruption appropriate?

2. Empathy –Why was this call so important to them? Did the official demonstrate empathy?

3. Asking - Did the official ask any questions (if they needed to) of the player or coach to clarify why they were disputing the call?

4. Paraphrasing - Did the official use the paraphrase tactic to clarify what the coach or player was saying. Did they use the tactic as a sword to interrupt the coach or player without generating more resistance?

5. Summarize – Did the official summarize to create decisiveness and provide a common ground of understanding or points of disagreement?

6. How would the group have handled it differently?

7. Are there any other observations that have not been discussed?

Give each group 4 to 5 minutes to discuss their observations. Reconvene the class and have one person from each group present their group's observations to the class.

Redirections

Redirections are a tool to deflect side issues, verbal abuse or disruptive behaviors so that you can generate voluntary compliance, cooperation or even collaboration.

Who Do You Represent? - Divide the class into groups of 4 or 5 (depending on class size). Ask them "Who do you represent when you officiate?" You can clarify the question by asking them who would be ashamed of them if they were seen on social media behaving unprofessionally during a game. Have the groups discuss this question for 4 to 5 minutes. Have one person in the group record the answers. Then have each group present their answers to the class.

Name Your Weakness - Ask the officials in the group to share experiences regarding verbal abuse and disruptive behavior. You can also ask them to share the things that are said to them that would make them angry. Point out to them that this would be their weakness that could cause them to act unprofessionally. Then discuss how to name the weakness so they can control that weakness.

Redirect Abuse – Create a script for redirecting verbal abuse or disruptive behavior relative to the sport you officiate. Follow the steps listed in the Appendix to conduct this drill. This drill can be conducted utilizing the Triad Training concept. You can also add the tactics utilized in the drills conducted for the 10-5-2 rule and the Stop Sign drill.

Example of a Redirection Script:

Coach Comment:

"*He's traveling! He moved his pivot foot! Get in the game, you're better than that!*"

Official Response:

"*Coach, I did not see him move his pivot. I had a good look at it.*"

Ethical Interventions

These drills are designed for an official to intervene if or when their partner(s) may act unprofessionally.

Divide your officials into groups of three. Official #1 plays the role of the player or coach who is agitating the other official. Official #2 plays the role of the official that loses control and begins to act unprofessionally. Official #3 steps in and removes official #2 from the area and takes over the conversation with the player and or coach. Each official should practice the role of Official #3.

Example of an Ethical Intervention Script:

Player Comment (while walking away):

"You have been struggling all day!"

Official #2 Comment (while rapidly walking toward the player):

"Really, how about you stinking up the court!"

Official #3 Comment (moving in between the official and the player):

"Jim, I've got this. Go back to half court."

Persuasion

When you encounter sustained resistance and it is still appropriate to talk, you need a tactic to resolve the situation. You first need to develop a persuasion script that is practical and relevant to the sport you officiate. Once this script is designed you can conduct the drills use the steps discussed in the Appendix.

Persuasion Tactic:

1. Ask (coach or player what the issue is or ask them to do something);
2. Set Context (explain rule and/or call);
3. Give Options (good, bad, back to good);
4. Confirm non-compliance (they won't do what you are asking);
5. Take Appropriate Actions (ejections/restrictions/cards).

Example of a Persuasion Script:

1. Umpire: "*Coach, what's the issue?*"

   Coach: "*He tagged him on the back. I saw it from over there!*"

2. Umpire: "*Yes he did tag him on the back but the runner reached the base before the tag.*"

   Coach: "*That's not what I saw. He had the tag before he was on the base.*"

3. Umpire: "*Coach, I understand you don't agree with the call. This is a good game, so let's get you back in the dugout so we can get going.*" Pause and wait for response.

   Coach: "*This is ridiculous. You kicked that call.*"

   Umpire: "*Coach, if you don't leave the field I'm going to eject you. I don't want to do that. Work with me here.*"

   Coach: "*That's the second call you guys missed today!*"

4. Umpire: "*Coach, is there anything I can do to get you back into the dugout?*"

5. Coach: "*Yeah, you can change the call!*"

6. Umpire: "*Coach, you're ejected.*"

When Words Alone Fail

These activities and drills are designed to assist the officials in determining when to take action that includes ejections and/or sanctions during a game. It also assists them in justifying their actions to their superiors.

Was the Ejection or Sanction Warranted and Why? - To create an activity for this section you can utilize a video taken from social media that depicts a situation in which a player or coach has been ejected or received a sanction for their behavior during a game.

Divide the officials into groups of 4 to 5 (depending on class size) and have them watch the video. Have them answer these questions:

1. Did the behavior of the player or coach present a situation of danger to you, your partners, other players, other coaches or any other people at the game?
2. Did the player or coach say or do something that warranted the actions? If so, what did they say or do?
3. Was it clearly inappropriate for the official to continue talking to the player or coach? If so, why?

Have them discuss these questions for 4 to 5 minutes and have one person record the observations. Then have one person from each group present their group's observations to the class.

Take Appropriate Action Drill – Divide your officials into groups of 3 utilizing the Triad Training concept. Use the script designed for the Persuasion tactic. Perform the script to the end and then have the official eject or sanction the player or coach. This meets the criteria that the Persuasion tactic has not worked.

A second approach to this drill is to inject inappropriate language and or behavior on behalf of the player or coach during the Persuasion tactics. This can be done in steps 1 through 4. It would be behavior that clearly would leave the official with no discretion but to eject or sanction. Make sure that this drill is conducted safely. Limit the physical contact.

Review and Reporting

The drill in this section is designed to enhance debriefing skills for the officials. You can divide your officials into groups relative to how many officials work during a game. Use the drills that are performed during their training and have them debrief the drills. One official should be appointed the head or lead official (crew chief, head referee). Then have him or her conduct a debriefing in the following manner:

1. Conduct a "wellness check" by asking if everyone is O.K.
2. Ask each official how they did.
3. Have each official describe what they saw during the game.
4. Tell them what you saw in yourself and what you saw of them.
5. Have each official discuss what they would have done different (if anything).
6. Summarize what everyone just talked about, while emphasizing how we can be better.

About the Author

Pete Jaskulski has been umpiring baseball in Wisconsin at the high school and collegiate level since 1981, receiving the Ken Kirby umpire of the year award in 2006 from the Wisconsin Baseball Coaches Association. He has umpired the spring state baseball tournament four times, three as a crew chief. In his training with the Wisconsin Umpires Association, Pete focuses on effective communications and game management. In 2014, Pete won the Wisconsin Umpires Association Umpire of the Year award.

Pete currently works as a training consultant for Vistelar where he travels around the country providing instruction to various professions in Verbal Defense and Influence (VDI), a training program focused on how to communicate effectively in the midst of stress. He has led many workshops for sports officials on how to apply VDI to officiating.

Pete is married to his wife, Pam, who was a collegiate soccer player. He has two children; Alex, a collegiate baseball player now working as a graduate assistant baseball coach and high school baseball coach and Kayla who is a multi-sport athlete (soccer, basketball, softball).

Pete retired from the Milwaukee County Sheriff's Office at the rank of Captain after 24 years of service and he currently holds the position of Assistant Fire Chief for the Village of Hales Corners, which he has been with since 1981.

Awards, Accomplishments and Recognition:

- Umpired on the high school and collegiate level (DI, DII and DII) since 1981;
- Umpired in both the spring and summer WIAA Sectionals since 1990;
- Umpired in the WIAA State Tournament in the spring of 2004, 2005, 2010 and 2015;
- Crew chief in 11 WIAA sectionals;
- Crew chief in the 2005, 2010 and 2015 WIAA State Spring Baseball Tournaments;
- Umpired in the following conferences: Classic 8, Greater Metro, North Shore, Southeast, Wisconsin Little Ten and the Woodland;
- Wisconsin Umpires Association: trainer concentrating on game management and communications skills;
- Recipient of the Ken Kirby Umpire of the Year Award in 2005, Given by the Wisconsin Baseball Coaches Association;
- Recipient of the Wisconsin Umpires Association Umpire of the Year Award in 2014.

Request for Reviews

Thank you for reading my book! I really value your feedback so it would be great if you could find the time to write a review on Amazon.

Send Us Your Peace Story

Now that you've learned how to keep peace during game, hopefully you've been able to use the skills you've learned.

If so, I'd love to hear your story.

To submit a story, please visit:

www.ConfidenceInConflict.com/peacestories

More Confidence in Conflict

Now that you have an understanding of what Confidence in Conflict means for sports officials, please watch for other books in this series:

Confidence in Conflict For ...

- **Everyday Life**
- **Campus Life**
- **Healthcare Professionals**
- **Public Safety Professionals**
- **The Workplace**
- **Youth Educators**
- **The Bullied Child**

Members of Vistelar's team of consultants hail from a variety of professions. By synthesizing our conflict management strategies with what really happens in real life, we can help you be "confident in conflict."

To see which books are available and release dates for future books, please visit www.ConfidenceInConflict.com.

Note: While you're on the site, be sure to sign up for the weekly newsletter. It's filled with free lessons and updates for Confidence in Conflict.

Learning Opportunities with Vistelar

Speaking

In-Person Training

Online Learning

Vistelar is a global consulting and training organization focused on addressing the entire spectrum of human conflict – from interpersonal discord, verbal abuse and bullying – to crisis communications, assault and physical violence.

Vistelar clients include all organizations where human conflict has a high prevalence, within business, health care, education, public safety and government.

Our primary purpose is to keep people safe by teaching them how to prevent conflict from occurring, verbally de-escalate conflict if it occurs and physically defend themselves if attacked.

Vistelar provides its training via a national network of consultants and speakers, training partners in specific market segments and digital training programs (online courses, DVDs, webinars). This world class network uses Emotionally Safe Performance-Driven Instruction™, a unique approach to training that emphasizes student interaction, real-world simulations, skill practice, memorable stories and physical activity.

Learn more at Vistelar.com

Made in the USA
San Bernardino, CA
06 March 2016